# A Guide Dog
# For The Thick

## by Terry Doe

PUBLISHED BY

# A GUIDE DOG FOR THE THICK

text © Terry Doe

Further copies of this book may be ordered by visiting the Publishers website
www.calmproductions.com
or by telephoning our mail order hotline 0845 4082606

Unit 4, Ashton Gate, Ashton Road, Harold Hill, Romford, Essex. RM3 8UF

Tel: 01708 379777 Fax: 01708 379979
email: mpa@mpressltd.com
ISDN: 01708 377698

*This book is dedicated to my mother and father, whose love and kindness knows no limits*

# Contents

# Introduction

First, thank you so much for buying this book. That is, of course, if you have bought it and you're not reading this after borrowing the book from someone. Perhaps you've been given it as a present, which is perfectly fine of course. In that case please pass on my thanks to whoever had the good taste to furnish you with such a gift. As for you 'borrower' types, you'll have to deal with your guilt as best you can.

Anyway, welcome to A Guide Dog For The Thick, which I hope you'll enjoy and tell everyone else about. Without letting them borrow your copy of course, because we've already learned that this would be just plain wrong. Let them buy their own. Be firm; it's probably the only language these people understand.

Back to the book, then, and some reading advice. This book wasn't designed to be read in one sitting, or even several substantial sittings. This is a small sitting book into which you may delve as the mood takes you. It's perfect for your holiday suitcase, and each article has been crafted to represent a safe sunbathing session in Benidorm or Bournemouth on a clear day in late July. This book is also ideal for your tasteful loo-library, where its easily managed pages and wipe-clean cover offer obvious advantages.

As I write, Morris prefers to poke his head onto my lap and dribble. How pleasant for me.

Within these pages you'll find life with Morris laid bare for your amusement. Well that's the idea at least, so feel free to snigger at my misfortune should the need arise. I'm used to people sniggering at me, you know. Oh yes, Morris has kept me in sniggering potential from the day he blinked his piggy little eyes against the brightness of our porch light when we first brought him home all those years ago.

To be fair to him, Morris has also maintained an unceasing supply of love, loyalty and affection and, despite the occasional impression the following pages may give, he is dearly loved and we couldn't contemplate life without him. Erm...mostly.

Before I hand you over to the rest of the book, I'd like to say a special thank-you to Beverly Cuddy, the editor, proprietor and Guiding Lightess of the wonderful Dogs Today magazine. It was Beverly who gave me the chance to expose Morris's doings and without her kindness and encouragement, my torment would have remained private. Beverly is a special, talented, caring and ever-so-slightly scary person and I have Herself's full permission to express my love and admiration for her.

That's it, then, off you go. Take care, and remember to cuddle your dog, cat, children and each other every day. Don't cuddle your goldfish, though, because they hate it.

All the best from Morris and me.

Terry

# A Guide Dog For The Thick

## The very first Morris article...and nearly the last...

The guide dog and the thick bloke- a perfect match.

You are not allowed to say 'thick' any more. All creatures with a mental capacity below the common whelk, are now to be referred to as 'intellectually challenged'. This is no help to me at all. One needs to classify one's dog Morris, and one wants to be correct. The use of the term 'challenged' indicates a forthcoming struggle, after which my dog presumably has a chance of emerging victorious. Not a prayer. There is simply no 'challenge' to offer. He is totally, irreversibly, dense.

To be fair, Morris was never expected to represent his species at Oxbridge and first impressions confirm a physical, rather than cerebral bent. He is a bull-terrier; i.e. white, barrel-chested, and pig-faced, with compulsory patch over right eye. Stunningly beautiful to me, hideously malformed to those who prefer pets without egg-shaped heads and high-profile pink testicles. We all know what Bull-Terriers were bred to do, and given half a chance, Morris would probably do it with gusto, but he has been denied an amateur boxing career, so he isn't punch-drunk -- he's thick. There I've said it again.

At the pre-purchase interview with Morris's Mumsie and Dadda (don't blame me, this was how they introduced themselves), I had the chance to observe his biological parents. I distinctly remember the male as daft, with fluorescent-pink testicles; Morris is simply a chip off the old blockhead. Through misty eyes and indulgent smiles, the custodians of my puppy explained the behaviour of his dad.

Stupid? Are you kidding? He wasn't stupid, although I could be forgiven for my lack of perception. Morris's dad was having me on. He does this a lot, clever old bugger. Apparently, hurtling down the stairs and banging head first into the radiator, was desperately witty. Leaping in the air and landing flat on his back, every time the telephone rang, was another trait possessed only by the truly gifted.

He also dipped his nose into a mug of scalding tea, during my first encounter with the family, and would have continued dipping until his snout was par-boiled, had Morris's other dad not shut him in the kitchen.

I believe I was expected to finish the tea, but somehow didn't fancy it. I had contemplated plunging my nostrils even deeper than the canine mastermind had, thereby displaying awesome intelligence, but declined on the grounds that there were enough deluded people in that lounge as it was.

I was struck by the serious nature of the interrogation. All family details were demanded and considered. I must have impressed them, and their devotion certainly impressed me, so we arranged another meeting. This time Morris's entire collection of parents, were to meet my wife and kids. I hoped we were worthy. Perhaps I'd better start teaching the children how to head-butt radiators.

We passed. We'd been judged and found suitable. Baby Morris was bundled in his blanket and presented by his non-biological parents. Before we left, Morris's dad confirmed his sharpness by flipping an entire trayful of tea over himself, impressing my wife no-end. I told her he was going for the sympathy vote. She reckoned I was as potty as the breeders. I wasn't potty. I was having her on. I do this a lot.

Morris on the other hand, is thick. Father was a contender, but son has taken dopiness to Olympic level.

He very nearly killed me a while back. Being a robust little chap, he needs to be physically drained on a regular basis, or mischief floods his empty head. I yomp him around nearby Staines Moor every day, taking in the sights and sounds of the Great British countryside, plus a few electricity pylons and the odd railway line. Anyway, we enjoy it, and the land is flat enough for me to spot incoming dogs long before Morris does.

This incidentally, is the way to recognise the seasoned Bull-Terrier owner. Look for 'periscope neck' syndrome. Eyes constantly scanning the horizon, as though watching a tennis game in slow-motion. It works. Morris has yet to engage, despite the irresponsible attitude of some owners, who see me put Morris on his lead and assume I've just admitted he is a canicidal maniac.

# A Guide Dog For The Thick

He isn't. He growls a lot, snarls sometimes and generally acts macho when approached by strange dogs. Morris has his inner circle of hairy chums, never curling a lip at any of them, but these are regular Moors-goers, he has had time to get to know them. I'm not really sure he'd latch on to a strange dog, and as I'm not about to experiment with his reputation, or someone else's pet, I'll stick to my combat-avoidance scheme.

So don't think we share our homes with a killer, because evasive action is taken. While you are at it, please don't allow your dog to sniff our dogs' bits and generally wind them up, while we become human maypoles, in an effort to keep the peace. Thank you.

Right, back to Morris trying to kill me. On the Moor grazes every herbivore imaginable. Morris looks at horses, cows and sheep with commendable disregard. He is not a worrier. He doesn't really have enough to worry with to be honest. If too much interest is aroused--perhaps a cow feels her calf is in danger of catching Clueless Bull-Terrier Disease from Morris--I let out with my famous "Cooomonin'enboyeee!" and he does just that, usually cannoning into my legs and laying me out. At least he comes to call, there are those who will not, but we never gossip.

On the day of near death, the Moor was fog-bound. Goody. Less bit sniffing dogs to worry about. Morris and I strolled together, visibility down to a hundred yards or so. Kind of eerie, punctuated by the periodic bellow of a bored ruminant, its location disguised by the blanket of fog.

Morris went A.W.O.L. for thirty seconds, only to reappear hotly pursued by an enraged yak. The yak wasn't a yak, it was one of those hairy, ginger, Scottish jobs which adorn the labels of whiskey bottles; it was unfortunately, bloody mad. Quite what Morris had done to freak the yak out, was a mystery, and would remain so if Jock McYak had anything to do with it. This thing weighed two tons in its stockinged feet, with a dirty big pair of amber javelins at the focal point. We are talking serious horns here. Considering he was almost an H.G.V., the monster showed a blinding turn of speed.

Morris had yet to work out that the yak intended to make terrier pate out of him, and bounced along merrily, a severe goring closing by the second. Then Morris spied me, cowering behind an anorexic hawthorn shrub. He homed in like a not-very-smart bomb, tracked passionately by the last of the European bison. Obviously, I was going to die. Morris would bowl me over as usual, then I would be trundled upon by the yak, punctured a few times, and tossed about a bit, until I lodged lifeless, half-way up a pylon.

There were ten nano-seconds of my earthly reign remaining when my survival mechanism switched to auto pilot. Poking my head through the token

All that stood between me and a charging yak.

bush, I delivered the following command with every decibel of my manly bearing.

"BaarggerOrrrfYoooowaaah!" This impressive demonstration of vocal control ended in a paroxysm of coughing, as my lungs imploded and fell in bits down the front of my welly.

As traditional breathing returned, three things were apparent. Firstly, I wasn't completely dead. Secondly, Morris was capering around my bush without a blemish. If this were not enough, the ginger yeti was lowtailing it back to the highlands at warp four. Apart from the swollen blood vessels in my eyes turning the fog pink, everything was normal once more. As a celebration of our good fortune, I searched frantically for something blunt to batter Morris with.

He can do some things extremely well. Reducing boating shoes to saliva coated flip-flops, is his party piece. He only eats the uppers, and even then the toe-cap usually remains, so it's not as if they are unwearable. I consulted an expert. She told me something was lacking in his diet. While I ransack every pet shop in Europe for boating shoe extract, Morris cruises the house on permanent alert for the real thing.

I can handle him. He was not invited into our home to play chess, or entertain us with after-dinner speeches. Morris is our best mate. He does his job with limitless loyalty, affection and trust, plus an infectious appetite for fun, which tolerates neither mood nor sulk. No, we're not thick, just happy. We've been having you on. We do this a lot.

# Fleas A Crowd

## Morris bugs the entire household...

Morris, our immensely dense bull-terrier, has elevated himself. His appearance in this journal, has triggered a change of outlook. Morris is now the canine representative of St. Francis.

He began the canonisation process, by collecting hedgehogs. It was late summer, a time when tradition instructs Mrs. Tiggywinkles everywhere to abandon their offspring. This hoggette must have had a genuine stud for a husband and a womb like Earls Court, because she'd managed to produce, and offload, at least six of her kids in our back garden.

Last year when Morris was mortal, he scoffed a hedgehog - spines n' all. It must have taken some serious swallowing but he's a trier is Morris. He soon learned that you can't keep a good hedgehog down, and chose to regurgitate it along with half a gallon of bile, over my record collection. Pink Floyd weren't, and the Beatles' White Album was a sort of textured green with hedgehog relish. Hedgehogs were removed from Morris's list of doggy treats forthwith, only to re-appear twelve months later as the focus of his new found spirituality.

The actual night the leaf turned over was hot, so Morris crashed out in the conservatory. He has a lovely bed there, composed of personally-chewed wicker, with a doggy-duvet to raise the snuggle factor. I left the conservatory door open to cool Morris's slumbers and to allow him unlimited widdles in the back garden. There's an enormous wall around our garden. Only Himalayan cats with oxygen gear even attempt to climb it and most of them hear Morris crashing through the undergrowth and decide against a visit.

Not Mrs. Tigg apparently. She came, she dropped the sprogs, she trundled off. Morris must have come over all Wilberforce, collected the waifs, before they had time to become strays, and filled his bed with them. Plonking himself on top of that lot must have brought a few tears to the undercarriage, but my Morris is not one to allow mere torture to thwart a new-found destiny.

Bedtime. I closed the conservatory doors and bid Morris goodnight in response to the thump-thump of his loyal tail. All was at peace. Our children had been sub-contracted to their grandparents for the week-end, so I only had the state of the economy, global warming and the current form of the England cricket team to worry about before dozing off. Have to say, even the public flaying of our lads by those unsporting Aussies, would have been elbowed from my list of concerns, had I known that Morris was sharing his bed with a half-hundredweight of assorted vermin.

Guess what I found, when I went to collect the morning mail? Overnight, our conservatory had become the first UK branch of 'Fleas 'R' Us'. Morris was a'thrash with the hideous creatures. I could see them leisurely backstroking through his coat, before holding their noses and diving for breakfast. The importers of the plague, lay snoring in Morris's bed, no doubt grateful for the reduction of their irritating burden.

Wife alert! Herself was trundling around upstairs. I knew it would only take three minutes for her to shift from bleary, to ballistic. A raving cleanliness freak, she'd only just agreed to stop hoovering-up defenceless spiders, on my solemn vow that I'd throw the big ones outside twice a day until they learned to poo in the shrubbery. We live in Surrey for God's sake. You can't have parasites in Surrey. Estate agents have the parasite franchise in Surrey. One glimpse of the tidal-wave of ticks, lice and hopping filth, currently flowing through our conservatory, and my wife would beat me to death. With Morris.

*STEP-ONE.* Isolate dog.
Run to rear of conservatory, open door and hook Morris out with walking-stick. Prod dopey git toward kids' paddling pool, thankfully still full, and hoik him in. Threaten castration with garden hoe if he dares move.

*STEP-TWO.* Stall Herself.
Tell her there's a spider at large downstairs that looks like a cross between an octopus and Godzilla. If she'd care to drift back between the covers, I'll give it a couple of body slams and kick it toward the nearest hydrangea. Top tactic, she retreats.

*STEP-THREE.* Evict lousy lodgers.
Using same walking stick, up-end dog bed and roll defensively-postured hoglings into cardboard box. Resist urge to employ walking stick as five-iron, and chip Morris's little mates back over bloody garden wall where they belong. Sneakily release the Addlestone Six in neighbour's garden. They've got a couple of acres and grow their own herbs. They'd probably be grateful for a set of free-range slug scoffers.

*STEP-FOUR.* Ransack shed to prepare for chemical warfare.
Sod the ozone-layer, organic ideology and goodwill to all living things. Anything that deals death, is aimed through the conservatory door and unleashed.

I deployed 2 puff-packs of ant powder, an entire can of something called 'Stay-Kill', every last squirt of fly killer, and a two-litre canister of industrial strength hairspray, which smells like tear-gas and exhibits the properties of atomised

Superglue. With our conservatory about as welcoming as the staff canteen at Chernoble, my attention is returned to St. Morris the Wretched.

Bull Terriers have a unique talent for looking guilty. Nothing is more pathetic than a downcast downface. It may have snuck an unauthorised tidbit from the kitchen bin, or chewed its way through a supporting wall, the look will be the same. Morris had his look on now. Standing rigid in the paddling-pool, head down, tail clamped, even a tremble from his muscle-bound legs. The piggy eyes pleaded for mercy.
'Not a prayer, you walking safari park. You've blown it this time matey'.

Insecticidal shampoo was dripped on him from a flea-proof distance, until he was bright green and slimy. Then, I took the squeegee-mop to him, until he erupted into a foaming heap. Morris looked like a sheep designed by a council committee. Not for long though. I de-foamed him via the hosepipe. I'd broken every 'green' creed in the book, with my chemical blitzkrieg in the conservatory, so I might as well go the whole hedgehog and defy the hosepipe ban.

Foamed and rinsed thrice, two flea-collars bolted to his neck and clouds of powder announcing his arrival ten seconds before he became visible, Morris was adjudged suitable for re-entry into polite society. The conservatory was vacuumed to within an inch of its life and the tubs of pot-pourri revitalised with essential oils to mask the aftermath of armageddon. Devouring my entire supply of luck for the next three years, fate had allowed the wifemeister to go back to sleep and miss Morris's little flea-asco completely.

We got away with it - that time. Less than a week later, Morris tried the same trick with a baby rat. Its mummy didn't like her charming child being rat-knapped, and went toe-to-toe with Morris over five rounds, from the conservatory, though the dining-room and on to the lounge. I wasn't there. Herself was. It was still my fault. Anyone want to buy a house in Surrey?

# Burning Issue

## Chim-chimera, chim-chimnea, chim-chim-cheroo…

I'm lovin' my chimera and I won't give it up.

Like most middle-aged men, I need my toys. Due to my forced co-operation in a reckless breeding program which resulted in three teenagers, I have no money for sports cars, boats, or similar vehicles of indulgence. The addition of a Morris-shaped bull terrier to my financial burden means that most months I can barely afford my counseling costs but, by now I'm too far gone to mind so I make do. I've still managed to wangle a new toy, though.

Herself has bought me a chimera, or a chiminea, depending upon which pretentious garden centre you buy it from. To the handful of unenlightened readers, a chimera/chiminea is a sort of freestanding, pot-bellied fire of Mexican origin, usually made of clay and designed to provide outdoor warmth and crude cooking opportunities for those that prefer to ignore perfectly serviceable kitchens. There's more to a chimera/chiminea than that, though – especially when you have one that lives in the same bit of world as Morris.

Mine isn't any old chimera/chiminea, either. It's a cast iron one that can't be shattered when knocked about as Morris charges around the garden. It also won't be frost-bitten or, more to the point, Morris-bitten. It burns logs, charcoal, coke that looks like donkey poo, and pretty much anything else I can sneak into it when Herself's out and I want to experiment with fire like I did when I was a kid. Having a chimera/chiminea entitles me to a log pile and (glory of glories) an axe with which to chop firewood.

Morris and I now spend hours sprawled before our chimera/chiminea, he enjoying the concrete comfort of the patio slabs, me on my favourite garden chair, glass of red wine in hand and stockinged feet tucked under Morris's fat bod while my mind melds with the flames. Morris doesn't have a mind in the recognized sense, so he's allowed to chew logs and sniff around the log pile for non-existent mice while I prod the fire with a stick to change the channel on flame TV. Only the truly in-flamed can know the glory of independent fire worship.

# A Guide Dog For The Thick

Morris thinks he co-owns the chimera/chiminea and cocks his leg against it on a regular basis to confirm this fact. I don't bother because I've got the receipt. So, my dalliance with al-fresco fire is always enjoyed in tandem with Morris. When the log-splitting season rolls around and I'm happily flailing away with the axe, it makes sense for Morris to be safely locked up. Axes are expensive after all, and if I axe-idently (geddit?) hit Morris with my new one, it could certainly break. And no, Ms. Bonkerslady from Brighton that writes me those strange letters – I didn't mean that really.

Locking up Morris whilst I enjoy chimera/chiminea-realated activities within earshot of him doesn't work on all sorts of levels. As the willing axe chomps into each log, Morris throws himself merrily at the patio doors in that way that only brain-dead bull terriers can. He looks surprised each time the toughened glass bounces him back and obviously believes that persistence will be its own reward. So he keeps on colliding, increasing his terminal velocity in line with the stubbornness of the patio door. This can only end in tears, and they'll be mine, so I shift Morris to his run while I finish my essential chopping.

No good. Morris can hear every thunk of the axe and now turns his attentions to the door that's keeping him from chimera/chiminea heaven. When the door fails to implode, Morris just stands there and barks. Then he barks a bit more. Then he really barks, until I've had enough and the neighbours are tutting in that outraged manner that Surrey residents have made their own. So I have to stop chopping logs and start lighting the chimera/chiminea. At the first whiff of woodsmoke, Morris knows I'm indulging in fire-fun without him and the barking starts again. Such not fun.

You see, as with everything else in my life, I have to consider Morris's stance on my chimera/chiminea inspired doings. It's not fair. I had to surrender my strimmer because Morris certainly would have snuck up and poked his stupid face in it while it was flaying weeds. My jet-wash had to go just because Morris hated it. He saw my jetwash as a vile, vomiting hoover and gnawed its wand into oblivion one day when Herself and I were considering a mechanical mulcher. We then decided against the mulcher on the grounds that somehow, some way, Morris would plunge his head into it while it was turned on. He spoils all my fun, Morris does.

By some sort of miracle, Morris has yet to leap into the fiery belly of the chimera/chiminea. Truth to tell, he's not even peed up it when it's still hot, so there's hope for a fried Morris-free future as we speak. I'm being all sorts of staunch about my chimera/chiminea and there's no way I'm getting rid of it. Total supervision and perhaps an electric cattle-prod may well be required to keep Morris from disappearing up the chimera/chimimea – shaddup Ms. Bonkerslady – but I'll do whatever it takes to hang on to it. For, in the burning building that Morris has made of my life – I really do need a fire escape.

# Bully Tart Anyone?

## Oh look, Morris is a crash-test dummy...

You know how all bull terriers are all ruff-tuff, roister-doister, macho types that laugh in the face of pain and cock their mighty legs against all degrees of agony? No? Mine neither. What's going on there, then?

Morris, in common with his breed, is indeed 90% tank. The problem is, he's also 10% tart. The former allows him to crash through previously solid objects, fall off high things, head-butt walls, trees and assorted immovables and generally blunder through life inside his natural flak jacket without so much as a squeak. The latter 10%, however, compels him to shriek like a scalded queen if you tweak his toenails, or, heaven forbid, he gets a thorn in his tootsie. I say again – what's all that about?

Example. Morris recently ran full-speed down the bank of a reservoir and discovered that the laws of momentum also applied to him. His legs couldn't keep pace with basic physics, thus he became a hairy snowball, which immediately evolved into a one-dog avalanche which hit a small but unreasonable tree. The impact could be heard throughout most of Berkshire and even those with houses beneath the Heathrow flightpath poked heads out of windows and exclaimed "Blimey – that was a loud one!"

I was convinced that Morris was at least dead, and I would have to bear home his broken body a-weeping and a-wailing with traditional grief. In fact, it was the tree that required a bit of resuscitation,  and despite my best efforts, its anti-sheep, mesh protector tube-jobby just couldn't be saved. Whilst I hurriedly re-vertical'd the tree and vainly tried to un-bend the mesh, Morris took his unscathed self off to snaffle a gobful of sheep poo. A detailed physical examination of my dog revealed neither scratch nor scrape and it wasn't until my hand brushed lightly against his toenail that he whimpered with the pain of it all.

Now, contrast that, with this. Last week, Morris stuck his stupid face into an ants' nest. I'm a bit of a whiz on what goes on in the natural world and I can spot the homes of ants, bees, wasps and most rightful occupants long before Morris ever gets a chance to evict any and get himself stung in the process. Alert as ever, I hoiked Morris away from the impressive, hi-rise ant heap – complete with hanging gardens of grass and a ragwort feature – before he was swarmed-at. One particularly valiant ant managed to unload its bum-bay of formic acid onto Morris's lip, but I considered my dog to have escaped lightly given that the heap contained millions of ants and therefore at least a pint of bottom-acid.

# A Guide Dog For The Thick

Well, you'd have thought that Morris had been harpooned. Per-lease! There was pawing-at-the-face going on all over the place, interspersed with rubbing-of-the-head-along-the-ground and even a bit of thrash-wiggling on the back with legs in the air. This was set to a soundtrack of bleats and yowls to which only those undergoing non-anaesthetised dental work are entitled.

"Get up you bloody poof!" I muttered, as Morris once more thrashed the thrash of the pantomime dying swan, amid snorts of imaginary pain and yet more pawing and ground rubbing. And please don't think me unsympathetic, here. I know my dog and his foibles only too well, and I also knew exactly how this melodrama would end. Sure enough, as soon as Morris spotted something worthy of his attention, in this case nothing more than a well-widdled-on litter bin, he forgot his immense trauma and went for a sniff. What a total tart he is.

He even tried to milk the ant incident when we reached home, doing his floppy-eared poorly doggy act to anyone mug enough to fall for it. Strangely, only extended scratching, petting and general fussing seemed to release Morris from his acid-bath hell, although the constant, propeller-like wagging of his tail gave the game away somewhat. Obviously, I was having none of it and told the mugs that they were only reinforcing Morris's tart-like tendencies. Just as obviously, I was completely ignored as, one after the other my lot indulged the hairy fool with all sorts of rewards.

The question remains; why do these dogs brush off real pain so lightly, yet go into girly mode with the minor stuff? Has it something to do with their original makeup and the hideous 'sport' for which they were invented? If that were so, though, how do we explain the tarty bit? I wonder if it's possible that these dogs have a sort of cut-off switch that's activated by pain. Perhaps only trivial traumas fail to trip the switch, leaving our dogs to enjoy playing the drama-queen in full non-discomfort.

Could be, you know. In fact, if that cut-off mechanism went a bit technical it could also exclude other impulses such as learning, logic and acquired intelligence, couldn't it? It could you know. Ladies and gentlemen – I do believe the mists surrounding Morris are finally clearing…

# Got Them Ol' Blue Bully Blues

## Where Morris has a bad hair dye...

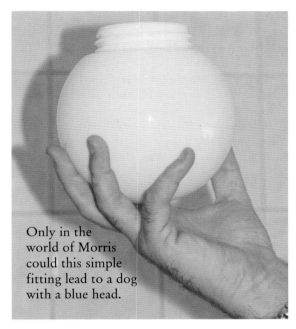

Only in the world of Morris could this simple fitting lead to a dog with a blue head.

I worry a lot, you know. Well, if you didn't know, you do now. Anyway, the fact is, lots of stuff concerns me, probably because I'm so worldly wise and so deeply, deeply aware of really important global issues. Take my hanging baskets, for instance. Not once, but twice now, I've stepped out of an early morn, green fingers flexed and itching to dead-head my dangly petunias, and what do I find? Scrunched-up cans of Special Brew and an empty bottle of Fosters Ice 'planted' where once busy lizzie and lobelia so gaily trailed.

That's the worry of living within yob-staggering range of the pub. Add the fact that Herself fired a three-second salvo of Mr bloody Sheen point-blank into my CD player during one of her domestic blitzkriegs, and that the reception of Channel 5 is not quite as sharp as the first broadcast from the surface of the moon, and that there's a dirty big rip in the brand new roofing felt on the shed, and... well, anyone can see how much I've got to deal with.

Yet, the one thing I never ever worry about is where the next article about my winkle-brained dog is coming from. Really, I don't. My Morris churns out inspirational acts at the cock of a leg. Here's his latest:

The light bulb in the bathroom went 'tink' when I tugged on the cord. Just change it, no big deal, okay? At least it wouldn't have been, had Herself not spotted a dead moth and a sprinkling of dried gnats in the upside-down white fishbowl that is our bathroom lampshade. Under orders, I unscrew the shade, which Herself somehow contrives to smash while scouring it clean of late insects. Fine. That's a trip to Do It All for me, then.

# A Guide Dog For The Thick

The new shade doesn't fit, so I buy a whole mounting bracket thingy, which is slightly smaller than the old version and leaves a ring of unpainted ceiling on show. I paint this bit of unpainted ceiling, turning it into a bit of freshly painted ceiling which makes the rest of the ceiling look like the one in the snug of Ye Olde Rat and Ferret. Now I'm commissioned to paint the entire ceiling, which then shames the rest of the bathroom and forces me into a total refurbishment. All because a moth and a few of his fluttery mates upped and died in our lampshade.

How is this all linked to Morris committing yet another act of lunacy? Be patient   we'll get there. While I scrubbed, sanded, brushed and rollered the bathroom, Herself dumped its chemical contents into a large cardboard box. All of the bio-degraded (and a few downright unstable) roll-ons and squirty things were then separated from the still usable deodorants, cleansers and wart lotions, lobbed into a bin bag, and slung out for the refuse collectors - so called, because they refuse to collect anything unless you drop them a tenner.

Still waiting for Morris to make his move? Well, wait no longer. As I laboured to turn our bathroom into a stylish haven of bodily cleanliness, Morris had his hairy paw through the bars of our front gate and was dragging the bag of discarded toiletries toward him. Morris, like all Bull Terriers, is hellishly strong, and lacks the intelligence to be anything other than single-minded. Thus it was that he eventually succeeded in snagging the bin-bag, ripping it open and chomping on the first thing that fell to mouth.

To viciously paraphrase Humphrey Bogart - of all the tins, in all the world, Morris had to puncture the one aerosol with 'Halloween Freeeky-Blue Instant Hair Tint' in it. My boys had used this muck to 'vampirise' themselves during trick-or-treat last year, and I'd banned it next morning, due to it staining the shower curtain and turning the grouting purple. The can exploded like a grenade in Morris's jaws, instantly spraying his head an even shade of electric blue, which, true to the label on the can, could indeed be called 'Freeeky'.

Herself certainly freeeked when Morris blundered into the house and started to offload the irksome dye by rubbing himself up and down the lounge carpet. Guess who got first use of the newly done-out bathroom? And indeed, guess who had to re-paint the blue bits? Oh well, at least I got this article out of it, and Herself got a newly-decorated bathroom. Morris just got a blue head, but he seemed happy enough. Then again, he doesn't have to worry himself to death over everything, does he?

# Canicidal Maniac

## Can he chew it? Yes, he can...

Tell me, gentle reader, when your dog wishes to inform you that he or she is a tad peckish, what little mannerisms are employed to ensure you get the message? Does your dog give the food bowl a suggestive nudge or two, or perhaps the cupboard wherein the doggy scoff lies may receive a tap-tap of a clever paw?

Guess what my Morris does. He bites canned goods in half. That's really in half. One can, bitten in two, to the accompaniment of the joyful slurping-out of whatever's inside it. Once he slurped a can of shaving foam. Another memorable bout of canned slurpage involved a tin of button mushrooms, an economy-size can of custard powder and a farm fresh container of motor oil - Castrol GTX I think it was.

That's more than acceptably weird, even for a mono-braincelled bull terrier, but the really spooky facet of Morris's misdoings with canned produce, is the fact that his proper food sits inches away from him protected by nothing more daunting than a paper sack. Run that by yourself again. Morris wishes to show me that he's hungry. So, instead of poking his pink piggy snout into his bag of Bakers Complete Mix, which would take a painless, stress-free five seconds, he chooses instead to steal a can of Lord knows what from God knows where, and chew it in half.

The process of mangling the can usually creates an unholy mess which varies in degrees of catastrophe according to the contents. Thus, the aftermath from a tinny of new potatoes won't always cause Herself to reach for a divorce lawyer, whereas the anointing of our house via a gurtbigfatfamilysize barrel of baked beans in perma-stain tomato sauce, now that's worth an application to The Jerry Springer Show for inclusion in the 'I Want To Hire A Hitman' episode.
In a pathetic attempt to balance the books in favour of Morris, I have to say that he's been his own victim on occasion. I distinctly remember telling you all (well some of you, what with reader rotation and all that) about the time Morris chomped the aerosol of Halloween hair colour and turned blue for a week or two. That was funny. Even Herself laughed at that one, mainly because the spray can burst outside and Morris was the only casualty.

Only last week, Morris shot himself in the foot when Herself had just installed a brand-new tin of Vanilla & Peach anti-pong combat spray in the loo. When deployed, the smell of this stuff prompts in me jumbled recollections of old fashioned sweet shops, the tiny bakery in the village where I grew up and the odd chapel of rest. Immediately apres-squirt, the assault on the senses is something our riot police should definitely look into, which should come as no surprise when you consider that Vanilla & Peach (with a bijou hint-ette of CS gas and napalm, I bet) has been concocted to overpower the stench of the modern teenager using the bog.

Anyway, Morris decided that the finest way to inform us that he'd like another meal, was to blag the new can of Vanilla & Peach, skulk off under my desk and give it the old canine crunch treatment. We heard the "pop-hiiiissssssshhhhhh" from the sitting room, as the aerosol burst and gave Morris a throat and nasal spray he'll never forget. By the time we got to Morris he was wretching from his toenails upwards, while the punctured can was still writhing around on the floor ejecting scented riot vapour all over my office. "Yoooooour problem.", said Herself, grabbing car keys and handbag, en-route to shopping therapy. And it was my problem, obviously. After all, it was me that bit the can of Vanilla & Mustard Bloody Gas, wasn't it? 'Course it was.

After laughing a lot and checking that Morris was OK, my three sons abandoned me in favour of some electronic space-death game round their mate's house and I was left to mop up Morris's mess. The most deja of vus swept over me as I reprised my role as the living, swabbing, apologist for my dog. Even Morris left me to it, no doubt tired out by his can-busting efforts.

Now then, here's a thing. How to get rid of the smell of super-concentrated Vanilla & Peach? You see, the clever gits at Lever Brothers, Johnson & Thingy and whoever makes Domestos can come up with all sorts of gear to mask the aroma of cooked fish, nicotine addicts, sweaty armpits and even junk-food reliant teenagers, but nobody's invented anything that overcomes the smell of the smell that overcomes all of those other smells, have they? No they haven't, trust me. I've spotted a loophole in the market, haven't I? Clever me, ay?

Meanwhile back in the primevally-urged world of Morris, he actually shows signs of changing his ways on the using a chewed-up can as a dinner bell issue. Only the other day he completely ignored an alluring tin of Ambrosia creamed rice that Herself had left unguarded on the dining room table for over half an hour. Eschewing, rather than a'chewing the can, Morris opted instead for the healthy, fibre filled pages of our youngest's Collins School Dictionary (updated edition). Most of the words Herself used shortly after discovering what Morris had done to the dictionary, could never be found within its pages, updated or not. Morris was unfazed and merely waddled off to his kennel to digest the meaning of life - plus several thousand other words. I was left to clear up, again. Never mind, it could be worse. Just think - you could own Morris.

# Canine Able

## A Biblical epic...

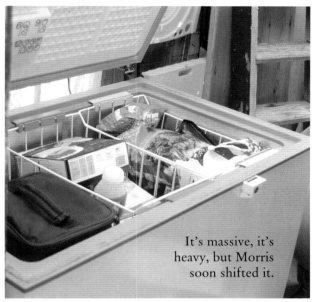

It's massive, it's heavy, but Morris soon shifted it.

And the Lord spake unto Terry, saying, "Oi, Tel-Boy! (for they were on first-name terms) Throughout thy life ye shall never have it easy, nor shall ye win the lottery nor profiteth from any ancient relatives popping their clogs and leaving ye a right tidy dollop of cash. Neither shall ye be free of hassles from double glazing vendors or tele-sales gits who shall phone on Friday evenings to announce that 'our representatives are in your area and would like to offer you a free consultation'. And I don't have to justify any of this, for I am the Almighty God who created the heaven and the earth - including the tricky bits like the Grand Canyon and Milton Keynes - and you are but a lowly scribe who owns a dog that dear old St. Francis himself would surely have strangled with his bare hands." And lo, it came to pass that every time Terry droppeth his toast, verily it landeth buttered side down, usually after smearing the crutch of his best trousers with Marmite.

So that explains the 'why me Lord?' when stuff always happens to me. That's why my dog is a delinquent and that's why my three children will probably go on to de-stabilise a government or two. Well at least it isn't my fault.

I had a serious 'why me?' day only last week. First, some scumbag in a skip lorry thought my car would look better with a crease down one side, and duly donated one free of charge - free of any charge to him at least, seeing as the driver took his job literally and skipped-off sharpish. Then the sofa expired. After three years solid service as a trampoline, coin bank and hider of carpet stains, the left arm fell off when our eldest stood on it to get a sticky dart off the ceiling. There's handy. I'm nearly two-grand down and it's not even lunchtime.

# A Guide Dog For The Thick

As the main distributor for disasters in the Doe household, Morris thought it was time he got in on the act, and after rubbing both of his brain cells together he came up with a masterstroke. Morris disconnected the freezer. That's the big freezer that lives in the shed. The very freezer that Herself had newly de-frosted and stocked to the gunwales with all manner of expensive nutrition, most of it being designer grub from Marks and Sparks.

We didn't discover Morris's contribution to the 'why me' day until the next morning, when junior Doe skipped down to the shed to pluck a raft of frozen waffles for his breakfast treat. Except the waffles weren't frozen at all. The waffles were all limp and drippy - as was I after Herself had finished screaming.

Morris was bang to rights on this one. He had prised the freezer from its specially built alcove to get at a feather duster Herself uses to drive away spiders. The feather duster is kept handy down the side of the freezer and Herself wields it like Zorro's sword to parry and thrust her way toward another successful burger-gathering trip. Morris has longed to mangle the feather duster for years and his chance came when someone (probably God) left the shed door open. Bulldozing aside the freezer, which when full and frosty only weighs as much as a Ford Mondeo, Morris dislodged the plug and started a major meltdown.

Incriminating evidence found right behind the displaced freezer, included the slobbery remains of a plastic handle, with the odd purple feather still clinging pathetically to it. The emergence of bits of purple plume in Morris's poo confirmed what we already knew, and the Good Lord had done me up yet again. But neither he, nor Morris had finished with me yet.

Herself had stormed off to get some shopping therapy, leaving me to scrape out the dead freezer's bowels and dispose of the contents. Never a wasteful person, I cooked up a heap of defrosted un-re-freezables and once the kids were groaning under the weight of bar-b-qued sausages, fish fingers and Cornetto's, I gave the rest to Morris. He had himself a pile of stewing steak, garnished with three prawn vol-au-vents and most of a Wall's Vienetta.

By the time the female volcano had gone sufficiently dormant to return to the fold, all was normal in the Doe sitting room - well apart from the one-armed sofa. Just as the sneer had finally faded from Herself's lips, in waddles Morris and pukes up a fine mound of feathery steak all over Herself's handbag. Nice one God.

I wonder if Buddha beats up his subjects like this? Maybe I could give that nice Harry Krishna a call. Perhaps it's time to start sacrificing animals? I bet Herself has a suggestion for that one.

# Postman's Knack

## Morris involves me in a parcel farce...

'I SEXUALLY ASSAULTED THE POSTMAN - AND IT'S ALL MY DOG'S FAULT!'

Tragically, the above statement does not announce Jerry Springer's latest exhibition of maladjusted humanoids. It's a statement of fact. I have assaulted the postie. The attack was directed at a part of him that is often used for sexual purposes - and I swear by Almighty God, that it was absolutely the bloody fault of that hairy git of a dog of mine.

Oh, I'm the one who's laying awake nights, expecting the old bill to boot the door in at any minute. And it's me who fully expects to be carted off to Newgate gallows, thereby to hang by my bits until I, or they, fall off. But, as countless innocent men have cried before me, ' I ain't done nuffin' Guv'nor - honest I ain't.' In anticipation of your launching a global, 'Free The Addlestone One!', campaign, here's what happened.

Crufts started it off. I attended on bull terrier day and three times made my footsore way to the splendidly spotty Dogs Today stand. There, on each occasion, I was completely ignored by my previously esteemed (not now matey-girl) editor, who was allegedly off being famous on the telly all over the place. So, I went away to sulk among the bull terrier folk and their superb exhibits. After basking among the bullies for an hour, I'd almost forgotten about my cruel treatment at the hands of this magazine's Obersturmfuhrer, and was engaged in happy chat with a kind lady who told me that she 'really, really loved the Morris articles'. I was just thinking that I'd record what this blessed soul was saying, for later playback to our own darling of the media, when another lady approached us and doubled my fan club at a stroke.

I loved it, I did. Each splendid (and most attractive, may I say) woman sought to outdo the other with kindly compliments. Anyone with an ounce of class would have blushed to their boots and writhed in embarrassment under this hail of approval. Not me. Certainly not. I kept reminding the ladies about various Morris episodes, which sparked off fresh waves of incoming appreciation. I wasn't so much fishing for compliments, as deep-water trawling.

This flattery-fest culminated in an offer from my first fan, which the second one took as a challenge. No, not that kind of offer. I was to be presented with a hand-knitted jumper, which turned into two jumpers the instant that fan number two sussed that she was being outdone and matched the offer.

# A Guide Dog For The Thick

Even I was feeling a tad toe-curly by this time, although not sufficiently so to withhold my address, of course. After fielding just one more blissful salvo of appreciation, I left Crufts, smiling the smile of one who is about to acquire a brace of wooly-pullies. Of course, I tried a final, pathetic attempt to hook up with La Cuddy, but quelle surprise, she was auditioning for Wish You Were Here, or something, so I went home in as much of a huff as anyone with two fine jumpers to their credit, could muster.

Spookily, both jumpers arrived on the same morning, along with the usual stack of wasted trees in junk mail form. The bundle was so large and squishy, that my small and compact postie had to carry it with one hand on top of the pile and one below. I went to relieve him of this burden, and seeing that I am six-foot four, he stood on tiptoe to present the stack to me at a more convenient height. Being a courteous and postman-appreciative fellow, myself, at the same time, I went low on my parcel grab stance. Thus, instead of connecting securely with the parcel pile with my lower hand - I grabbed the postie's crutch. Got me a fine handful, too, I did.

"Whoah-up!" shouted postie, backing off hurriedly - and who could blame him - as he dropped a shower of Royal Mail on my doorstep. I went purple and spluttered repeated apologies to his retreating front, due mainly to the fact that he wouldn't turn his back on me until he'd reached the safety of his van. I'm sure there was more fear than pain in that man's eyes, when my hand closed on his …er…'male-pouch'.

So that's me down as a raving bloody pervert, then. I have to blame Morris, because without him I'd have never written these articles, then those lovely women would not have made me jumpers, the postman wouldn't have delivered them - and I wouldn't have grabbed his crutch. Morris, it must be said, has got me again.

# Computer Crash

## Morris goes a byte too far...

You see, if the bits that hold a table together are eaten – it tends not to hold together.

Start with the biggest thing you can think of. Double it. Add a sprinkling of bull elephants, stick on a Wembley Stadium, then increase it by the amount of worry the Queen's children have caused their mother during the past ten years or so. Now, which ever way you look at it, that's pretty big isn't it? Well it isn't anywhere near as big as the trouble Morris is in right now.

I'm powerless to help him, for his punishment is being dealt with by a much higher authority. This is due to the fact that of all the people Morris chose to commit an atrocity against - he went and did Herself. Got her big-time too, but he's paying for it now.

It's painful to watch, and I know what Morris is going through because I've had some of it. Herself has a scowl that can strip paint. When she purses those lips and narrows her eyes into slashes of smouldering green, squaring padded shoulders and exhaling forcibly through flared nostrils - Herself looks spookily like a King Cobra. Then, the talon of a finger points to Morris and she hisses, 'Sssyou! Gettt outtt offf myyy siiiightt!' Fair makes me shudder to describe it. Morris gets this on every eye-contact, and he'll keep getting it for at least a month I'm thinking.

So, now you're wondering what can any one dog do, to earn such a punishment. Especially a dog with such an amusing catalogue of calamities to his credit. Here's what happened.

Because Morris is useless and despite months of alleged training from me (so he's my fault when it suits Herself) he still tries to climb into the underwear of visiting females, and because we were invaded by Herself's P.T.A. henchpersons - Morris was banged-up in my office for the duration of their visit.

# A Guide Dog For The Thick

Hearing peals of Liebfraumilch-inspired laughter, Morris probably felt a tad miffed at doing solitary, while a posse of guffawing grannies had a right good chortle in his house. When Morris sulks, he doesn't do it passively. He amuses himself.

Next morning, with me gathered safely off to work, Herself planted herself at my computer to make official the piddly outpourings of the previous night's 'Committee meeting'. Instead of a tasteful portrait of Homer Simpson appearing on the computer screen, surrounded as he usually is by clickable icons - all she got was a swarm of hieroglyphics and a load of electronic blinking, as the screen repeatedly died and was yet re-born.

We've had computer trouble before and Herself knew that a swift and highly technical jiggle of the connecting cables sometimes did the trick. She went jiggle, jiggle, jiggle, her jiggling becoming more brisk at the irritating lack of success. Somewhere around the fifth bit of jigglage an explosion rent the office air, to the tune of, 'BWOPP!', followed by that sinister smell of electricalness on the melt.

Turned out that Morris had 'amused himself' by gnawing-up the main power cable to the computer and all that jiggling had literally blown it. After the cursing and screaming subsided, Morris was condemned to rot in his kennel and Herself popped out to get a new computer cable, a mere 18 miles away. Upon her return, my resourceful partner re-plugged-in the computer and created her vital documents without a hitch - until she tried to print them and discovered that Morris had also mangled the printer cable.

More screaming, this time at a frequency miles above the threshold of pain, had to be followed by another 36-mile visit to PC World. This would be Herself's last cable replacement, because she'd checked for further damage and had even removed the remaining cables so that Morris couldn't attack them in her absence - he having been granted a temporary stay in the office on account of rain.

She reached home once more, ushered Morris outside into 'his bit', and was plugging away merrily, when the entire computer crashed. No, not a 'computer crash', as in software on the blink. This was a real-time crash, as the formerly sturdy pine table which supports the computer and monitor fell to bits and dumped the whole heap of hardware on Herself. She was damn near avalanched to death by Packard Bell she was.

Have a wild guess as to why that table collapsed? Morris had pulled out all six of the wooden wedges which hold it together - that's why. A heap of incriminating splinters were found behind my desk. Morris is on death row and it will take at least a six-figure Lottery win to cheer Herself up enough to grant a reprieve.

Next issue, don't be surprised to see an article on flea-control where me and Morris once lived, OK?

# Open-Door Policy

## Well, at least he's trying...

He's laughing at us, you know.

After only several years, Morris has learned to bang on the door to tell us he wants to go outside for a widdle. Or a poo. Or to re-re-check that someone hasn't re-filled the food bowl that his coal shovel gob emptied in four seconds this morning. Or, indeed, to up-chuck the former contents of that bowl, because four seconds is about five minutes too fast to ingest a bowlful of food. But wait, I've lead you astray, here.

You see, by using the phrase 'bang on the door', I have given the impression that Morris will apply his willing paw to the door that opens on his run, where he widdles, and carries out his various food processes. This is what normal dogs do and you can certainly be forgiven for thinking that Morris takes the logical route. Sadly, he never has and it's fairly obvious that he never will.

Morris doesn't knock, scratch, bark or in any way indicate, at the door through which he wishes to go. No, instead, he belts the living hell out of the stable-type door that connects my office with the rest of the house. This is a sturdy door of impressive construction and split, as stable doors are wont to be, into two half-doors. The lower half of the door rattles impressively in its fitments when Morris pounds on it with his feet, head, shoulder and bum. Should Morris imagine that he has detected a cat, hedgehog, ant or shire horse in his run, he will then decide that the imagined creature is desperate to become his playmate. This makes him anxious to be outside with his new imaginary chum, so he launches himself at the door. You can't imagine the noise this produces.

Should the police ever choose to batter their way into my house, I shall not be intimidated by the noise of it all. Similarly, if, as I have been predicting for years now, my sons' chemical silo of hair products ever explodes, I'll raise an

He'll stand there all day, not knocking.

un-shocked eyebrow and merely mutter "told you so, din't I?", and carry on at my convenience. These things will not alarm me, because I've been drip-fed Morris's concussive requests to go outside. What does send waves of panic through me, is the prospect of re-training Morris to knock at the right door.

Training Morris to do anything he wasn't going to do anyway is not for the faint-hearted. Or the normal-hearted. In his puppyhood, which should be over any year soon, Morris was declared 'untrainable', albeit by a trainer with about as much empathy for dogs as I have for astrologists, feng shui'ers and anyone who really thinks Big Brother is a form of entertainment. In other words – none at all.

I've no desire, and even less expectation, to turn my dog into a point-perfect pooch that follows my every signal and slams down his bum to attention on the first 'ss' of ssit, but is it too much to ask for him to learn just a couple of constructive responses?

Short answer – Yes.

# Carnation Street

## Morris borders on vandalism...

Like most 'physical' dogs, my Morris loves, wants, and needs plenty of exercise. Having yet to learn how to pump iron, do step-aerobics or ride a bike, he gets his physical fix through mile after mile of traditional walkies.

I mix his walks in the same way I mix his food. Morris mostly gets to tackle a complete blend of rough and knobbly stuff, with a decent bit of greenery thrown in. Then, to balance things out I give him a session or two on ready-mix, as we do the rounds of our local streets. The second option really is the exercise equivalent of cheap tinned dogfood, because it's a straight 'in and out' job - with a fair chance of Morris getting a few short, sharp runs.

Urban dogwalking has its own charms and demands, especially when you choose over half a hundredweight of bull terrier as an accessory. If, like my fine self, you are further blessed with 6 foot 4 inches of bearded largeness, then you run a very real risk of being perceived as distinctly dodgy.

Try to allay the impression of latent thuggery, by smiling kindly at every living thing within beamy-face range, and you've just volunteered yourself as some sort of escapee. Same goes if you cross the road to prevent a tangle of leads between your dog and an elderly lady's arthritic corgie, which despite being so old it has to have its leg cocked for it - still fancies a raving tear-up with a bull terrier. Crossing that road is not regarded as responsible evasive action, but an admission of guilt, plus proof that neither you nor your dog should be out in polite society.

I've seen mums dart prams across busy roads, rather than meet me and Morris head-on. Even if I'm a' Sunday strollin' with my entire family, the picture of integrated cano-human happiness, there are those that gather small children to their skirts and stand defiant behind disapproving scowls, until Morris-the-loaded-gun walks safely out of firing range.

Us bull terrier owners do have a slightly harder time of it when out walking, though. How about when they (I'm referring to the dogs here) stop dead to sniff some intriguing secretion or other, while you stride on regardless? 'Ssscrruunch!', goes your shoulder joint, as it flirts with forcible dislocation, while the dopey mutt continues its impression of a dockside bollard. Then, all three of its brain cells spark up at once, and the realisation dawns that movement is required. From being an immovable object, your dog suddenly becomes that most mushing of Huskies - and once again your shoulder ligaments produce a sound like someone putting bubble-wrap through a mangle.

Recently, Morris and I had one of those, 'if only I'd had a camera' moments. Quick scene set. Two roads from me lives old Eric The Flowers. Eric's real surname is as dark and mysterious as the windows of his bungalow, but because he's Welsh and grows the most magnificent flowers, carnations mainly, he is known to one and all as Eric The Flowers. Now, Eric is an uni-talented kind of guy, in that the only thing he does well is gardening. On the inside, his bungalow is decorated in a style which could be labelled 'early grubby'. The rooms are strewn with horticultural paraphernalia, behind a decaying set of crocus-yellow net curtains, which began life as snowdrop white, at about the time the Beatles sang 'Strawberry Fields Forever'.

Protecting Eric's precious flora from unwelcome fauna was the ricketiest fence in Christendom, professionally braced at roughly 3 yard intervals with garden canes, hairy string and the moss of ages. Now old Eric spends his entire visible life in his front garden, and he always looks up from his dibbing, or pricking out, or whatever, to wipe away a dew-drop and make eye-contact with every passer by. He wants you to comment on his carnations and such like, which I'm always happy to do of course. Trouble is, as Morris and I are regulars, Eric feels safe in shuffling over to fish for more compliments about his garden.

One afternoon, I took Morris for an urban mooch along the usual route. Hailed by Eric's watery eyes, we pulled in to pay a toll of pleasantries, only to find that the old chap had no intention of letting us off so lightly. He had planted a dozen dwarf conifers that very morning and needed urgent assurance that such rashness would not undermine the very fabric of our neighbourhood.

As I nodded and smiled my way toward a polite break for freedom, Morris became impatient and sort of head-butted Eric's fence to relieve the tedium. In super-slow motion, watched by all three of us, a 20 foot section of Eric's bodged-up fence simply keeled over. Morris looked up at me as if I'd done it, and poor old Eric was rendered speechless by the sight of his beloved plants being smothered in a miscellaneous patchwork of green, slimy timber, tied up with string.

'Aw, bleed-nell', panted Eric The Flowers (between foul Welsh curses), as he struggled to hoist the fence off his namesake. By a supreme stroke of luck, the rag-tag barrier held together while we hauled it to its feet once more, after which Eric skilfully staked it by belting a broom handle into the ground and lashing the fence to it with his long-term unemployed washing line.

Strangely, whenever Morris and I saunter past Eric's pad lately, he never even looks up. That's OK, we don't mind really. Me and Morris aren't the sort to take a fence.

# Street Of Shame

## The sweet smell of sexcess…

When Morris doesn't want to move, that's pretty much the end of it.

I'm overjoyed to report that Morris hasn't embarrassed me at all this month. He's shown up my eldest son, instead. Which was a right larf, obviously. Strangely, my Kristopher entirely failed to see the funny side of it, but then he's at that that nouveau-shaving, pre-spotty stage, where he imagines that the whole of Surrey is judging his every move and holding up scorecards. If that's so, then Morris has just steered Kristopher to a fine set of minus-6's.

Kristopher has already begged me not to tell the world of his catastrophic loss of cool, and I've agreed to consider his wishes. More importantly for my son's development, I've decided to teach Kristopher once and for all that I never break a promise. Oh yes. I promised that I'd get him back for smashing my shed window, so here goes.

Kristopher sometimes takes Morris out for an extra-curricular stroll around the neighbourhood. His mother imagines that our beloved boy has come over all angelic and is contributing to the essential practice of Morris-depleting. A depleted Morris is a far more acceptable item to have barging around a house than the version with the industrial strength Duracell batteries with which we're normally blessed. Kristopher's dad (yes, me) knows his son. Was I not a gangly teenager myself? I could gangle-up a storm when I was Kristopher's age, and I know what he's up to. He's using Morris as a babe magnet.

Oi! You can stop that sniggering right now, you lot. For your information, Morris attracts loads of admirers, and some of them are perfectly normal people. When he's swaggering down the road in his posh leather harness, that self-assured smile bisecting his happy head and his bits all jiggling in time to the clickety-click of his two un-clippable toenails, Morris is practically irresistible.

Sure, the occasional Philistine gathers its children to its skirts and hurriedly crosses the road to avoid him but there's no accounting for such creatures, so we tend to swagger on regardless.

Anyway, Kristopher had trundled off with Morris en-route to collecting another sackful of style points while I was discussing the merits of rational expectations in macro-economics with Herself. OK, we were having a ruckette about me buying a more powerful pressure washer than the two we already have, when the telephone rang to sound the end of round one. It was Kristopher on his compulsory teenagers' mobile phone.

For our Kristopher, image is all. Morris doesn't agree.

"Dad. Pleeeease come and get Morris, he's well-showing me up, Dad. He's just laying in the middle of the pavement by the shops and he won't move! I've tried everything to get him up but he weighs a ton and he's blocking everyone's path. Some mad woman just swore at me because she had to push her pram into the road to get round him. Pleeeease come and get him, Dad, pleeeease!"

Naturally, I planned to hit the street at a run to salvage what I could of my lad's cred, yet swift though my response was, it wasn't anywhere near fast enough for Kristopher. Before I'd had time to lace up a second trainer, the 'phone rang again.

"Daaaaad! You've GOT to get here now! Morris's willy is hanging out and he still won't move, and he's howling and all that, Dad! Oooh Dad, run, pleeeease!"
I discovered that I don't do 'run', not even to prevent my son melting from shame. I did manage a dignified power-walk on Kristopher's behalf, though, and I must say that I felt flushed with the self-righteousness of healthy exercise when

I arrived at the scene. Kristopher was considerably more flushed than I, however, and appeared to be hopping from one foot to another and clenching most of his body in pure embarrassment. Bless him, in a pathetic bid to plug the massive leak in his pool of cool, he was pretending to talk to someone on his mobile. Morris, his scarlet winkle thrashing like a mad conductors' baton, still stood his ground and howled that soulful song I knew so well.

As soon as I was in range of Morris's lead, Kristopher slammed it into my hand, muttered something along the lines of "Awwww Gaaaawwwd, I'm moving out. I'm going!", and did just that as fast as his trembling legs would carry him. Morris barely noticed that he was the subject of a frenzied baton-change, preferring to sniff deeply at some magical, invisible substance he'd discovered on the pathway, re-charging his primeval urges for another mighty yowl. I knew in a second what was going on. Morris had chanced upon his favourite perfume - essence of in-season bitch - and the rest is primitive canine history.

Being over 30 and therefore bereft of cool, I had nothing to lose from this situation, so I simply wrapped my arm around Morris's point of balance and hoiked him off his feet. Carrying a love-lorn, fully-paunched and by now gyrating in hula-stylie bull terrier even a few yards was no mean feat, but I eventually managed to get Morris down wind of the bitch widdle. The instant he'd cleared his sinuses of girlie sex-invitation aroma, Morris reverted to his oblivious self. He even had the cheek to look first at his deflating willy and then to me, as if to ask "What on earth is THAT all about?"

Re-playing the incident in my mind, I couldn't help giggling as my dog and I walked toward home. Just as, in 20 years or so, my Kristopher will be able to laugh about it, too. Probably.

# It's An Ill Wind

## It's just the chives talkin'...

You can be reasonably sure a dog is spoiled, when you regularly drive him somewhere nice - to vomit. Morris is carted off, almost weekly these days, to up-chuck amid more harmonious surroundings. In fact, if I wasn't certain about his numbskull status, I'd get to thinking he was doing it deliberately to con an extra walkies out of me.

Come to think of it, Morris never starts his 'shoulders heaving, mouth agape, and "bloop-kaaark" noises routine', when my wife is in sole charge of him. And it wouldn't take even him long to suss that if he can catch my eye while browsing off the odd garden shrub, he's only a couple of pantomime retches away from a bonus trip in the car.

He would know that since he took up open-cast mining and I was forced to sell the back lawn into pavery, there's not a blade of grass to be seen, and constructing a vomit-ball now involves gulping variegated ivy and other toxic fronds. He'd also know I worry about him doing this, and the little git would certainly be aware of my extreme guilt in not providing him with proper grazing land.

Morris could be related to Pavlov's dog, and 'swallowing leaves equals walkies' might be lurching around inside his skull, along with, 'soon be time for my 27th puppyhood and a gnaw of that new chair-leg I've been promising myself'.

Of course Morris could actually be ill and his periodic puking merely a symptom of some lurking gastro-catastrophe. Except he isn't ill at all. I know he isn't, because the vet is getting fed-up with telling me this, and I'm in danger of being labelled a paranoid parent and "It's about time you realised Mr. Doe, that Morris is an habitual scavenger and continually eats things his body doesn't want, so his system gets rid of them in a perfectly natural way - ok?".

Admittedly, my dog's experiments with herbal emetics, produce nothing more than bits of masticated toy, sweet wrappers, hairbrush bristles and an occasional pebble. These are delivered entwined among whatever greenery Morris has chosen and bound with a revolting tracery of mucous. One second after he dumps this lot, he is off like a hare, presumably in celebration of his new-found fitness. This may very well be the canine equivalent of my childrens' ability to leap tall buildings within half an hour of being granted sick leave from school.

An occasional extra-curricular romp with Morris is no great burden, but there exists a more sinister side-effect to his scavenging, one which has seriously threatened my dog's tenancy agreement.

When Morris is fed, he reverts to wild dog type and rams as much inside him as he can, in the shortest possible time. Then he bloats to capacity on water, followed by a crash-out coma in his bed, to absorb all those expensive nutrients. This is fine by the rest of the family, who can now get those jobs done which Morris hinders when he's conscious. My wife can vacuum the carpet without Morris attacking the Hoover, my sons can play Monopoly on the floor, safe from having a bull terrier's bum plonked on Pall Mall while his other end snaffles half a dozen hotels, and I can prod my word-processor free from shouts of "Daaaad, come and get Morris puleeez!"

Unfortunately, not the slightest piece of peace will exist, should Morris scoff something that sparks off his 'little problem'. We are talking serious wind here. Flat-out, force-nine flatulence, of eye-watering intensity, caused by reaction between Morris's scheduled grub and the bits of free range muck he finds lying around the house. A bellyful of blameless doggy diet, can be turned into a silo of chemical weaponry by one nibble of the wrong tidbit. A single baked bean was once the catalyst for six hours of torture, hands waving in front of wincing faces and cries of "Oh gawd - not another one Morris."

When hurricane Morris hits, it takes no prisoners. Once, after I'd moistened his mix with onion gravy (I thought gravy would make it taste nicer, that's all) the eye of the storm visited our lounge and emptied it of all human life within 12 seconds. Morris fled soon after us, because he couldn't stand to be near him any more than we could.

Worst of all was the day my wife fed him, then left to buy a fresh sack of dog food. Meanwhile, I came home and found my poor puppy with no food in his bowl, nor was there any in the store cupboard. The emergency tin of 'Sloppity-Chunx' was emptied before him, and devoured in the customary three grabs. While I tut-tutted about how everything seems to be my responsibility these days, Morris raided a string bag of shallots I had hanging in the shed. He ate at least 5 large, lethal ones, before his coughing and spluttering brought me running to the rescue.

Too late. Morris's bomb-bay contained a double load of fermenting meat and mixer, plenty of vegetable protein and fibre, plus a stockpile of nature's finest fireworks. When the blue touch-paper eventually ignited, the effect was an out-of-body experience.

I defy anyone to remain loyal to a pet who barks at both ends, produces fumes which slay the hou15plants like a chemical scythe, and whose bottom-burps set off smoke alarms. Morris actually yelped at one point, as a waft of his own odour assailed his nostrils - either that, or it burned his bum on the way out.

Obviously, I was blamed for the entire episode and ordered to cart Morris away to his vomiting grounds until he'd run out of gas. Can you imagine what it was like to drive a car, filled to bursting with such a stranglesome blanket of shallot-driven foulness? Trust me, you can't. Had the police spotted a Citroen weaving down the road that night, with the driver gasping for dear life out of one window and a dog's bum thrust forcibly from the other, I'd have been breathalysed on the spot.

Morris was still exploding days later. After that lot, a shallot embargo was placed on our house, but the family were already shell-shocked and dived for the door if Morris so much as hiccuped. Still, if I ever need to manufacture a reason to scoot off for a few hours, I can always announce that Morris has just chomped on a pickled onion.

# Incapability Brown

## Morris takes garden leave of his senses...

The skilled tradesman's best friend. NOT!

We are being severely Ground Force'd at the moment. New, trellis-topped fence panels, reeking pleasantly of preservative, give comforting separation from our neighbours, while sacks of bark chippings await the scattering talents of my lavishly-funded experts. Block pavers with bums borrowed from builders squat like African tribeswomen, giving birth to inspired arrangements of pretend geology. It presents a fine tableaux of the modern garden industry, minus compulsory decking and water feature. The tableaux lapses into still-life a little too often for my liking, but then I'm only the bloke who's paying for it all, so what do I know?

Morris is a garden feature that everyone could do without, so I've banished him until the work has been completed and the opportunities for mischief have been reduced to bearable levels. I tried, briefly, to allow Morris to help the landscapers but he got the sack after just two days. To be precise, he got three sacks, all filled with compost (the peat-free, bog-friendly stuff, before you ask) which were disemboweled and their contents flung to all points of the new compass bird bath. Morris achieved this in the time it takes for our men to drink 'a quick cup of tea'. So that's about an hour, then.

The peat sacks represented Morris's written warning. He wasn't immediately dismissed for gross misconduct because he'd been left unsupervised, and also because the block pavers adore him. One of the pavers has a bully, and the main reason he became interested in the breed, was a meeting with Morris in our local pub. Morris was on top form that evening and snuggled, slavered and slept in a most endearing, and utterly false, cameo of what it's like to own a bull terrier. Many have been smitten by such displays, myself included, and few dogs can sucker a punter like a bully in 'look at me, love me' mode.

My own smittence - have I just invented a term? I do hope so - came when I attended my first bully gathering at one of the Ormandy shows at White Waltham. I'd read every breed-specific book I could get my hands on, but nothing had prepared me for the effect of being so close to dozens of show standard bull terriers. After ten minutes of slack-mouthed admiration I became snowblind from gazing at drifts of white-powdered muscularity, punctuated by outcrops of red and brindle. The perfect shapes of these dogs, their spirit projecting visibly as they posed for their public, and the impossible combination of mischief and dignity possessed by the Champions, had me enthralled. One day, when I met the required standard, I would own a bull terrier and he would be my friend for life. For once, that's pretty much how it turned out.

A Morris no–go zone.

Morris has his 'mischief and dignity' combination set all wrong, of course. Sadly, he copped a 50-to-one M and D ratio, and you'll not need me to tell you which bit is which in that little recipe. Eventually, even his adoring pavers had to admit defeat after the third broom-handle was splintered, although the writing was on the garden wall as soon as Morris chewed the fencers' new spirit-level. You could say he burst the bubble. His gardening career ended in banishment after a fraught 48 hours, less kipping and tea breaks. Then Morris found half a gallon of wood preservative that does what it says on the tin.

I'd bought the can of 'does what it says' stuff to protect the wooden shelfy-bits on the bar-b-que and to freshen-up a flaking bench that was taking the rustic motif a little too far for our new-look garden. Like me, Morris loves the smell of such things. Unlike me, after going in nose-first, Morris always follows up with a thorough chewing, to gain maximum pleasure from whatever he's found. When that happens to be a can of designer creosote, it's a case of 'God preserve us'.

Morris had just punctured the top rim of the tin when he was intercepted by one of his paver mates, who was easing himself back into the rigours of blockwork after a particularly demanding tea break. Morris hadn't had time to create anything artistic with the dribbling contents of the can, he merely spattered his paws, chest and an insignificant area of paving, which is due for a jet-wash anyway. As I said in the face of Herself's blistering scowl of disapproval, I think he looks nice in brown.

Morris scrubbed up as well as he ever does, and, as I reach the happy ending of this month's column, our garden threatens to look attractive for the first time in 10 years. It's somehow cost me the tearful part of three-grand, but, as far as Morris-based mayhem went, I reckon we got off lightly. Next up, re-building the porch and painting the house exterior. Ladies and gentlemen, the possibilities are endless and the odds of Morris not causing at least one major catastrophe are, frankly, nil. This time, I think I'd better budget for some counseling costs.

# Morris – Unplugged

## When dolt meets volts...

Before we start, I'd better catch you up on the gossip. Of course it's not gossip, because we'd never do that here, obviously, much, so we'll consider this a 'social news update'. Anyway, you know that Stick Insect woman I had a very slight spat with a few months back? You know, her with the many-hoisted face and fictitious birthdate declaration, well she's been in touch and she's not happy. Can't imagine why, can you?

Sticky accused me of 'reacting ferociously' to her comments about Morris being pointless, and defending my dog in a manner that was 'out of all proportion to what was merely her opinion.' Fair enough. We all have a right to express our opinions and I certainly expressed mine about her, so I'd say we were quits. Mind you, she reckons she'll never be visiting our house again, so I'll declare Morris and me the winners of this little exchange and leave it at that. She's still a rancid ol...(Terry's comments edited at this point for legal reasons).

What else. Oh yes, the blisteringly talented artist and sculptress, Alison Van Dyke, definitely wants to do a model of Morris. A live one, not a taken-from-photos jobby. This involves me delivering a more-live-than-Alison-could-possibly-imagine Morris to her studio, where she will capture his essence right there and then. Sadly, Alison can't possibly comprehend just how much essence Morris has and by the time he's infused her superbly appointed studio with it, I'm willing to bet she'll wish she'd never invited it in. It takes a lot to expunge even the temporary occupation of a dog such as Morris - at least a team of decorators and an exorcist, in my experience.

Alison told me that the last time a bull terrier had visited her for a sitting, the best she could do was to draw around the thing as it sprawled out on a sheet of card. Alison didn't mention anything about structural damage or nervous trauma, so I'd say she's in for a right laugh when Morris fetches up on her doorstep.

Next, I've been threatened by Becky Bailey, minder and henchperson to the editor of this very publication. Via a poison e-mail, Becky told me that my copy was so late that, not only had I better get that copy over sharpish, I'd better have a damn good excuse or I'd be sent to the Dogs Today sin bin and miss an issue. Oooooeeeeeoooo! As if I'd be afraid of Becky Bailey. I showed her who's the guv'ner, don't you worry. I made her wait for almost an hour before I sent my copy in. Sometimes you just gotta be firm with these people.

Last bit of news is that my wife is expecting quads and I've joined a troupe of nude mime artistes which embarks on a three-year tour of the Shetlands any day now. Or I could possibly have invented that last bit just to liven things up a tad. Same goes for Herself being all quadded-up in the womb department. Right, there's still time to in-fill you on what Morris has been up to since we last met, and I hope Alison's reading this - there are things in it she should know about.

Morris can now smell electricity. Either that, or he can hear it humming down the wires, or he's acquired an electro-magnetic bum. Whatever it is, it's serious and it looks like it won't be one of Morris's millions of passing penchants. My dog's flirtation with mains electricity has blossomed into a full-blown affair. Great, just what I need.

What happens is this; Morris detects the focal point of an electrical happening, such as a wall plug or socket, whereupon he waddles over and rubs his rear end all over it. Plugs, especially those sprouting from three-way adaptors, are not designed (and why should they be?) for use as anal scratching posts for bull terriers with no detectable brain activity. Thus, the plugs are dragged from their sockets and whatever was formerly plugged, becomes decidedly un-plugged.

This behaviour carries many potential risks, as I'm sure you can imagine. So far, our house has failed to burn down and Morris has yet to fry himself via 240-volts' worth of charge, but there have been casualties, oh yes. Herself found her new iron skidding rather than gliding over my underpants and it took her a while to suss that it wasn't my pants' fault at all, but Morris's plug removal regime that was the cause. You simply can't expect to flatten a 10 year-old pair of British Home Stores' finest with a cold iron, that's what I say. Morris has also un-plugged a hair drier whilst middle son was using it to heat-set his latest hairstyle, and more than one desperately important date with Lara Croft has been curtailed, when Morris disconnected the playstation.

I've been a victim, too, of course. Morris did his bum-shuffle number on the plugs to my computer, and the first version of what you're reading now went down the virtual drain. THAT'S why my copy was so late - see? D'you hear that, Becky Bailey? It wasn't my fault - it was Morris's, and you're welcome to put him in the DT sin bin for as long as you like. (That's me in the clear, then.)

# Gnaw Place Like Home

## Would chew believe it...

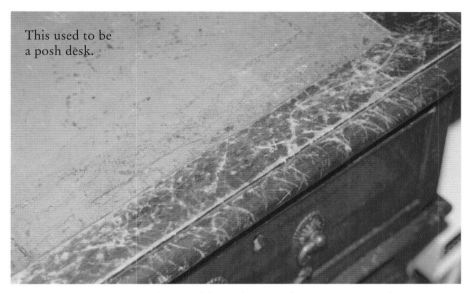

This used to be a posh desk.

When your dog has been designed from the jaws down, I guess it's fair to expect him to use them occasionally. Like all Bull Terriers, my Morris is anything but dentally-challenged, in fact when doggy-toy manufacturers print 'Virtually Indestructible' on their chewy things, what they really mean is 'totally indestructible - unless that bloody Morris latches on to it'. You see that JCB that was down your street the other day biting lumps out of the road? - that's Morris that is.

My dog's lamentably short C.V. only includes being famously stupid, breaking wind like a dyspeptic water buffalo and having a car-crusher where his mouth should be. Of these, the latter has been causing me some concern of late.

You see, when the most energetic member of your household is limited to the three talents already mentioned, life gets a tad fraught if he ever feels the need to express his annoyance. Truth to tell, Morris rarely gets involved in protests of any sort. Provided he gets his meagre daily minimum of several pounds of designer food, at least one ox thigh to chomp on, a sheaf of new bedding to replace the load he's just reduced to confetti, and a route march that would be rejected by the S.A.S. as being beyond the limits of human endurance - Morris hardly moans at all.

# A Guide Dog For The Thick

Inevitably in this life, such an easy truce can't possibly last and Morris and me are currently at loggerheads over something he wants to do, which I won't allow. It's not me at all really, it's Herself. She refuses flat-out to allow Morris to flop-out all over the soft furnishings, and because he's 'my dog' whenever he's out of order, I have to sort him out. Here's what I've tried so far.

*1.* Hoiking Morris off the couch and ordering him out of the room in my most assertive voice, whilst wagging my most assertive finger.
Result: He farts a couple of times and does his 'OK. If you won't let me do what I want - I'm going to run madly around the house until I knock something over', routine.

*2.* Sneaking up on him as he sprawls on his back in Herself's reclining armchair, muscly legs akimbo, snoring like a pig (which it has to be said, is a fair imitation of that particular chair's rightful occupant) then frightening the life out of him by walloping the arm of the chair with a rolled-up newspaper.
Result: A gigantic fear-fart, followed by 20 minutes of continual barking to cover Morris' embarrassment.

*3.* Discouraging access to sofa and chairs, by placing uncomfortable objects on them - knobbly books, mountain bike, gas cooker etc.
Result: Morris doesn't fart this time. Instead, he pulls all discouraging objects off the furniture and throws them around a bit, before climbing aboard. Then he farts.

*4.* Each time Morris is captured akip on the couch, I make him do half an hour's solitary outside in his kennel. Morris' kennel looks like the house Heidi grew up in, has fitted carpet and is filled with toys, so as a means of severe punishment it isn't really up to much.
Result: He sulks. Morris sulks by chewing the hell out of anything that will yield to half a ton of jaw pressure. I've discovered that most things we own will eventually yield to this.

To date, 'machine-gums Morris' has mangled, 1.5 expensive chair legs, his bed, a gate, the porch, our stair carpet, our stairs, other portions of chair, some garden hose attachments and sufficient footwear to fill a brace of wheely-bins. The ferocious efficiency of my dog's molars has to be seen to be believed, and even then most people don't believe it. I was watering the hanging baskets one day, chatting to my neighbour as I squirted, when Morris strolled past, wrapped his chompers around the hose in leisurely fashion - and just snipped it in half. "I don't believe that!", exclaimed my neighbour. And many have exclaimed the same, let me tell you.

OK, so my tactics to date have been less than successful. And before you start in with the suggestions about smearing every chewable item on our property with the patented anti-munch unction that deterred your wee Benjy when he was a pup, be assured that I've probably tried them all. When neat Tabasco sauce (I kid you not) is regarded as mere gate-garnish, and the slavering hound chews-on regardless, you know you are dealing with no ordinary dog. It is my considered opinion that nothing short of CS gas will have the slightest effect on Morris when he's in great white shark mode.

I remain hopeful, and would certainly try any sure-fire cures the learned readership cares to suggest, but right now I'm about as good at preventing Morris's oral-demolition of our world as I am at keeping his hi-visibility, Dralon-magnetic, white hairs off the furniture. Naturally, the entire situation is my fault and I've been sentenced to an undefined period of strategic nagging - as if I needed another demonstration of mouth power.

So here I am, caught in a withering, two-gob crossfire, between my partner and my pet. The way things are going, most of the white hairs being shed around this place are going to be mine.

# Ding-Dong The Witch Is Dead!

## Meet the un-stick'able stick insect...

"Well, what's the POINT of him, then?", said the skeletal, sneering woman in the too-young outfit and shiny, triple-lifted face. "I mean, if he's such a disaster, why don't you get rid of him and get a BETTER dog?"
"Like your husband did to you, you mean?"

Got the witch! Teach her to diss my dog. If there's any dog-dissin' to be done around my house, it'll be done by Herself - not some re-constituted reject from the Weybridge Divorcee Club's commando unit. Just because her husband finally came to his senses and offloaded her bile-spewing harpiness in favour of someone with a heart that isn't encased in permafrost, she thinks she can turn up her latest Harley Street nose at my poor Morris.

Well, you razor-hipped, collagen-lipped, boob-jobbed endorsement of the embalmers' art, Morris is still here, still loved and still happy. And he's not haunting wine bars and nightclubs on the trawl for a mug punter with the required rich enough / daft enough qualities to sustain a pointless lifestyle. Unlike you - you rancid old crab. Now, do me a favour and never drag your ex-foliated, colonically-irrigated, surgically certified carcase around to my house again, ever. Oh yes. Happy '49th' birthday for next week. Yeah, right.

Sorry about all that, dear readers. She needed that almost as much as I did. She's been trying to undermine Morris's tenancy for ages, ever since she invited herself around to discuss fundraising with Herself. That's my 'Herself', yeah? My Herself raises billions for local causes by bullying companies and concerns out of products, services and sometimes straight cash. Herself's brilliant at this and if it wasn't all in the name of charidee, she'd be done for demanding money with menaces.

Anyway, one evening, around stalks this Versace stick insect and within seconds she's grimacing at Morris and me whilst plucking white hairs from her designer denim with her 30-quid a finger false nails. Most of the hairs formerly belonged to Morris but I'm delighted to say that one or two were certainly mine, and never has my follicular free-fall been more enjoyable.

I mean, we live in a house with a dog in it for God's sake! It's SUPPOSED to have dog hairs all over it. If there were no dog hairs stuck to every furniture and fitting, we'd have to go out and buy some, or it wouldn't be right, would it? The stupid stick insect probably has an army of underpaid maids scouring every inch of her des-sodding-res four times an hour but this is a family home - and that means dog and Dad hairs.

Well, the first time Morris farted, such was the look of abject horror that you'd have thought Sticky was about to be ravaged by a particularly un-cultured gorilla, or even me. The meticulously strimmered brows were raised so high that I expected to see her de-bagged eyes overtake her forehead. Truth be told, Morris had unleashed a most impressive one. My boys and I were in fits. Herself and the Insect tried to pretend it wasn't happening at first, but when Morris launched a back-up, there was no denying it. Out came some ludicrously priced hankie, to be hosed down with repeated squirts of an alleged perfume that costs more than a small family car, the combination to be clamped over the new nose and lips until eau-de-Morris had dissipated. I wish she'd have let me clamp that hanky on her face. About ten minutes of total clampage would have done us all a favour.

After that first visit, Herself countered my disapproval of the creature-that-thinks -time-forgot-it, by telling me about the terrible wrongs its husband had supposedly done it. It seems that he'd traded-in old Sticky for a younger model - well, THERE'S a shock (not) - and was currently contesting her 'unbelievably reasonable' maintenance claims. According to what I'd already seen, Sticky was carrying at least 20-grand's worth of 'maintenance' as it was, what with all of her tucks, plucks and scrapings. I amused myself severely by picturing what would happen if her husband won the right to reclaim all of that investment. Imagine if Sticky had to hand back her enhancements. She'd look like a living time-lapse sequence. On the other hand, reversing a colonic doesn't bear thinking about. Make a good video, though. 'Ok, nurse - it's all gotta go back in. Switch the pump to 'blow' and stand well back!' Har, har.

Three more visits later and even Herself wanted rid of the Insect. Not as much as I did, though. Her sneering snobbishness, viscous rudeness and the spume of bitterness and unbridled hatred she ejected with every sentence gave me a migraine in minutes. Herself once asked if I could suggest a suitable male companion for Sticky. I told her that I had the perfect chap. "Who is it, then?", said Herself, the faint glow of hope lighting her still -attractive-without-surgery face. "Hannibal Lechter", I replied, and meant it.

Sticky is everything I detest, from the tips of her pedicured crone's toes, to the top of her empty, yet spite-filled, head. Imagine a bleached cross between a PMT'd Anne Robinson and a Daddy Long-Legs, with a face that has to be laced on every morning like a Victorian corset - and you're still nowhere near to knowing what a poisonous old baggage Sticky represents.

As one who always holds doors, chairs and coats for the glory that is womankind, such ungallant behavior as has been necessary to rid us of the She-Mantis, comes hard to me. But, dear, dear readers, for Morris and me, what sweet relief it has been. Yesssss!

# Caribee'n' Island!

## Bed-lam reigns…so no change there, then…

This bed has made my life so much more comfortable.

Morris rarely surprises me these days. He shocks the hell out of most people, and with a regularity that only a mono-braincell'ed bull terrier could achieve, but I like to consider myself immune to his bizarre habits. Somebody has to be, you see, or everyone around Morris would take on a permanently shell-shocked demeanour and we'd all stumble about like Valium testers on overtime. Yet, inoculate myself as I may, Morris still manages to pull a foible out of the hat on special occasions, just for my benefit and bewilderment.

The latest trip to quirksville concerns his bed. This was especially significant, because that bed represents the one and only triumph I have recorded since Morris came to occupy us. Regular readers may recall that finding this bed was, for me, of greater significance than discovering a new source of the Nile bubbling from the Holy Grail itself, in El Dorado town centre. By way of an unashamed plug, I'll name the superb product that has become known to me as the Caribee dog bed. That self-same combination of hi-performance synthetics that has somehow convinced Morris that chewing it isn't the way forward, and that pressure sores are so last-year.

Pre-Caribee, Morris ate every bed I bought him, and preferred to kip amongst the hardest, most sore-friendly surfaces his fat bod could be draped over. Since Caribeenisation has taken place, Morris's pressure sores have healed, grown hair and now exist only to impress girly dogs who Morris tries to kid that he's a rough, tough, outdoorsy type of guy. He isn't. He prefers to sleep on his blessed bed. At least he did, until one of my sons tried to use it as a trampoline. That bed is not a trampoline. So much not, that, it couldn't raise a single 'boing' when an unspecified poundage of daft teenager leapt on it and expected to be launched skyward. When I saw the dirty great hole in the centre of Morris's precious bed,

I was quite willing to supply a bit of skyward propelling myself, only none of my three would grass up the culprit. Being a bloke, I secretly approved of this show of solidarity, but it didn't help me with Morris's bed. With visions of born-again pressure sores sprouting by the dozen out of my dog's contact surfaces, I hit the 'phone at a run and begged Mr. Caribee for a replacement mattress.

Enjoying a particularly healthy run of sales, he was sold out, although one would be available in a week as soon as the new batch arrived. Until then, Morris could snuggle up on a doggy duvet or something, obviously. Obviously not. Deprived of his spiritual resting place, Morris went on sleep-strike, refusing to kip on anything but the hard, cold tiles of my office floor. To quote Del-Boy, it was deja-vu all over again. I put down carpet squares, blankets, my old coat and even the cushion from the seat that used to be Morris's favourite dream-chariot before the sacred bed brainwashed him. All avoided like plagues with rusty nails sticking out of them. Great. Just what I need, another worry about Morris.

He held out for three days, steadfast in his desire to re-grow his pressure sores. Then, I had a flash of inspiration. I wouldn't wait for the new Caribee mattress thingy to arrive, I'd improvise by stretching a blanket across the frame of the bed. Tah-naah! I hadn't the slightest idea how I was going to do this, but reality is never the first option in matters of Morris so I just lobbed a blanket onto the middle of the bed frame and went off in search of Caribee construction gear.
As if! I mean, what was I expecting to find that Morris hadn't already chewed or the boys had failed to scatter about the garden with all of my other tools? All I found was an ancient, congealed reel of gaffer tape and some bulldog clips whose springs had most definitely sprung.

Returning to stare at the bed for some sort of salvation, I was amazed to see Morris curled up on it. He was actually curled up on the blanket, his body completely through the hole in the mattress and surrounded by the bed frame. The bed played no supporting role in this whatsoever, save to satisfy Morris that he was still sleeping on it. And so it remained.

Provided whatever I wanted him to lie on had that non-functioning bed on all sides of it, it was fine. Morris's devotion to his skeletonised Caribee is as touching as it is pathetic. I've even caught him asleep in a sprawl, head on the bed frame, bum on the floor, rather than stretching out in perfect comfort somewhere else. As I say, it's pitifully touching. I'll take pitiful over painful any day, and so will Morris. But then, we are strange bedfellows, he and I.

# High Anxiety

## Morris seizes his window of opportunity...

Even in Morris's world of manufactured mayhem, he creates no more panic than when we can't find him. Nothing, but nothing, comes close to the explosion of dread, when the 'Morris is gone!' cry goes up. I swear, just typing those words has made my eyeballs sweat.

The 'missing Morris' syndrome afflicts our household on several levels, all stuffed with hideous visions. Most hideous by far, is the mental movie of Morris being abducted by the crawling filth that perpetuate dogfighting, when they'd be much better off exploring bungy-less jumping or sans-parachute skydiving. Mercifully, this video nasty is usually zapped by my cerebral censor and I'm left to worry myself sick over less perverted likelihoods.

In the past, Morris has shuffled off to enjoy a shoplifting spree, been apprehended by a council dogwarden and ended up in the fabulous care of the folks at Battersea Old Windsor, where he had a wonderful time while the rest of us head-butted walls to soothe our trauma. He's escaped only twice, or at least that's all memory will allow me to recall, but the horror of an unaccompanied walkabout remains an ever present threat to my sanity. Morris can cause civil war in the confines of our house, with five pairs of eyeballs watching his every move with justified suspicion. It takes little imagination to predict what could happen if he lumbered, un-checked into downtown Surrey. Well, the worst case scenario happened again the other day. I came home early from work, the house was empty, and there he was – gone. Before allowing the freak-out express to leave panic station under full steam, I am required to run a pre-trip check. I must first search the shed, lest Morris be asleep among the impossible clutter my family see fit to create in there. Morris once struck up a passionate liaison with a mouse that lived in the shed, and would sleep away endless vigils there in the hope that a half-ounce mouse would come out to play with a half-hundredweight bull terrier. It only took months for it to dawn on Morris that mice don't actually volunteer themselves for wrestling sessions with dogs more than a billion times bigger and thicker than themselves.

Morris wasn't in the shed. He also wasn't in the broom cupboard – a previous hide-out, made attractive by a passing infatuation with a feather duster – and he wasn't behind any sofas, chairs, bar-b-ques or cavity walls. The panic express was blowing a fine whistle by now, and steam was visible from most of its safety valves. I did the rounds of the family mobile phones. Herself had left the house only a few minutes before I'd arrived. She was in Iceland, stocking up on the sort of processed muck we wouldn't dream of feeding Morris. Herself told me that Morris was asleep in my office when she'd left. He'd raided the laundry basket and stolen my underpants, again, and she'd left him inhaling them in contentment. He couldn't be gone, she said.

I told her that he could, and in fact he BLOODY WELL WAS, Darling. Her phone battery must have died instantly. It does that when I raise my voice to it. Each of the boys' phones returned unhelpful grunting noises, all delivered through non-moving lips and translatable as 'Iyeno'. Great. Morris has evaporated, someone's beamed him up, he's been abducted by particularly stupid aliens and/or he's found a gap in the time-space continuum and he's on his way to disrupt the battle of Trafalgar, or annoy Hannibal's elephants. Alternatively, he could be on the roof.

Guess where he was. On the roof. Now why didn't I look there in the first place? How could I have failed to suss out that he'd been rootling around for more pants in my eldest's room and spotted an open window. In the world according to Morris, there's no point in having an open window if you're not going to throw yourself through it. So he did, and had the good fortune to drop only a yard and land on the flat roof that spans my office and the downstairs bathroom. This roof also supports our vital Sky TV dish, upon which, according to the adjacent puddles, Morris had widdled at least five times.

I'm sure I don't recall the Sky installation bloke recommending a gallon of bull terrier wee as a sure-fire maintenance regime, but our TV reception seems to have survived the deluge. Obviously, I was worried sick that those 'musicians' on MTV might have their talents diminished by urine-induced fuzz and crackle, but no such luck I'm afraid. Meanwhile, I was faced with reclaiming the widdler on the roof.

Thankfully, this required no more than waving a biscuit on my side of the window and assisting Morris's pathetic scramblings to hoik his fat bod back inside the house. He had roof pitch on his feet and bum, which stuck to the new carpet, the sight of which had Herself dropping her bags of Iceland's finest in shock as she, too, re-entered the house. All of which was my fault – but you'd guessed that bit already.

And now Morris and I are self-banished to my office to enjoy what passes for normality around here. I'm writing what you're now reading and Morris is still trying to get tidbits out of a Kong he emptied at least 30 minutes ago. All is well. Apart from Herself, that is. She's still hitting the roof. Been there, done that, thanks.

# Leggin' It

## There's trub in the pub when Morris does a runner...

The excitement continues here on Morris Island, where its namesake has done one of his impromptu walkabouts and the natives are revolting. For only the two-billionth time in his unpredictable life, Morris has pushed the tolerance envelope and landed himself in the naughty boys' chair. For, not only has he done a runner, he became bored with chomping the furniture – and chewed a hole in his own leg instead.

The hole began life as the site of the drip inserted by the vet during Morris' recent extremely serious non-illness. It was serious in that it cost me hundreds of pounds (although I never mention it) and required Morris to stay in dogspital overnight. Once he'd racked up enough tests to cost me the hundreds of pounds I never mention, Morris regained his normal, super-fit status. The vet's saline drip was removed, its pinprick covered with a fetching pink bandage and Morris was taken home to dream up his next misadventure. It didn't take him long.

Morris ate his bandage inside an hour and he began to worry at the drip hole with the perseverance that only extremely stupid bull terriers can muster. We mounted Morris-watch immediately, and distracted him with all sorts of ploys every time he attacked his leg but we merely delayed the inevitable. Within a day, the pinprick had been promoted to a crater and looked ripe for infection, due mainly to the impossibility of keeping any sort of dressing on Morris for more than 7 seconds.

He once had one of those plastic bucket-thingies fixed to his head, to stop him gnawing at some bit of his body or other. That tactic pretty much tops our list of 'things we'll never do again', hovering just below 'going on holiday with people we haven't known for at least 10 years'.

In the two hours Morris wore that bucket-thingy he turned into a mood-swung rhino with a side-order of bucking bronco. When yet another sideways thrash of Morris's bucketed head all but took out a patio door, I unclipped the thing and let stupidity take its course.

This time around, our worries about the crater in Morris's leg were relieved by the infinitely greater one fired by him sneaking out into the mad metropolis of Addlestone. He does this now and again, usually as a nasal-guided response to some whiffy bitch in heat. Basic life forms like Morris respond to their primitive urges as a matter of top priority, and once 'that' scent is sent, Morris has no choice but to heed its invitation.

Seconds after he'd heeded his primitives, up went the dreaded call "Where's Morris? Have you got him with you?" This sparks two pandas and a monium. Everyone in the house rushes around checking Morris's hidey-holes, calling his name and increasing the general stress levels with every 'Nope, he's not in the laundry basket...under the barbeque cover...on the roof" etc., until we realize that he really has slipped the perimeter defences and is at very large in unsuspecting Surrey.

The après runner routine is a thing to behold. Herself hits the phone and alerts the police and several local shops, friendly neighbours and anyone else she can think of who Morris may choose to visit during his illegal walkabout. I grab the nearest son, a spare collar and lead and set off on a power-walk, interrogating innocent bystanders as we go. Eldest son fires-up his car and practices the kerb-crawling version of my interrogation technique, although I have it on good authority that he seems to ask mainly attractive young ladies if they've 'seen a white dog hereabouts'.

Morris's latest expedition took a new twist when he struck out for a pub he'd never been taken to, due to its landlord's disapproval of dogs. I discovered his whereabouts when I broke a golden rule and made an enquiry of an obviously drunken man. He swayed, re-focused his one responsive eye, placed an affectionate hand on my shoulder and slurred. "If yamean a big bawterrya, 'ee's just crapped in The Crown, an' the Guvnor frew 'im out."

I thanked my still-swaying informant and set off at a dignified panic to The Crown, where a hasty enquiry showed that, after, indeed, doing a monstrous dump on the saloon bar carpet – and confirming for all time the landlord's stance against dogs - Morris had been temporarily adopted by a kindly couple who lived next-door to the pub. I knocked on their door, explained my mission and was re-united with the cause of it. While my accompanying son relayed the glad tidings via his mobile phone, I thanked Morris's hosts, who declared "Er...he's quite a handful, isn't he?" before bidding him goodbye with more than a hint of relief.

I'll be back to knock on that Morris-friendly door when this magazine is published and I'll present it, and a box of chocolates, to the kind folks who took pity on a disastrous dog and saved his owners from more hours of torment. I haven't worked out what to do for the landlord of the pub, but I'll come up with something fair and equitable. Unless I wimp out and just avoid the place altogether. I only hope (per-leeeease God) Morris does the same.

# Lourdes Of The Dunce

## Holy inappropriate...

Morris blessed my
office with a gallon of this.

My in-laws are Irish and after coming over to Surrey to breed, they've now retired to a tiny time-warp coastal village in the Emerald Isle. That means we don't see them as often as we'd like, my three boys are one set of grandparents down on the wisdom and guidance deal, plus, our free baby-sitting service has lost 50% of its staff. Selfish, I call it. Imagine transplanting to a spangly green corner of your homeland, where everyone has the time and inclination to stop for a chat, and you can see fishing boats and mountains from your kitchen window - when you already have the paradise that is Addlestone. Weird, but there you go.

Morris misses Grandma and grandpa, too. He misses them because, during every single baby-sitting stint they've ever done at our house, they used to feed him half of everything they had. In-laws have fish 'n chips - Morris gets half a cod and a wodge of fried 'taters. 'Phone up a pizza? Cut it in half and add a side order of garlic bread, then Morris can eat more than both in-laws combined.

Obviously, this stuff-Morris-on-demand regime was expressly forbidden by me, and just as obviously, my orders were ignored with the Irish philosophy of, 'Sure, doesn't the poor old fellah always look so sad if we don't give him a wee bit 'o food. My in-laws don't do 'wee bit of food.' They feed you so much, that, if your navel is an 'innee', it pops under the strain and becomes an 'outee', until your internal food mountain subsides. No wonder Morris is so fat. And me, come to that. And Herself's looking like a crowd of Kate Moss's all tied together, I notice. Good job I never mention it really.

So, that's the outlaws gone, then, and we all miss them terribly. Consequently, should Grandma request anything during her thrice-weekly telephone check-ins, it's treated like an order from the Almighty. Thus, heaven, earth and most of

Surrey are moved to accommodate Grandma's every whim. Her last whim was for holy water from the fountain at Lourdes. Apparently, she'd run out.

This request wasn't quite so bonkers as it first appears, due to my middle son, T.J. being down Lourdes way on his easter trip. T.J. - he's 'Terry Joseph' but Grandma christened him T.J. when he was about 12 minutes old, so there went my namesake - is hearing impaired and the marvelous people from the Handicapped Children's Pilgrimage Trust, asked him to join 5000 other young people on their annual visit to the world famous shrine in the foothills of the French Pyrenees. T.J.'s been before, he reckons it's 'well brilliant,' which any parent of the uncouth will tell you, is the bestest it ever gets.

Anyway, T.J. returned from Lourdes with, I kid you not, a GALLON of holy water. It didn't look all that holy in its plastic can, but the means to please Grandma had been secured, and that's holy enough for this house. After handing out presents to his family,   ( I got a Homer Simpson's Butt mousepad for my computer - cooool ) T.J. realised that Morris had been left out. Worse than that, Morris realised that Morris had been left out, and slunk off in slow motion to sulk. Do your dogs do that? Morris walks away at sub-slug pace, with many a backward glance, a calculated mime of 'Oh, don't worry about me, I'm nobody, after all.' We always make a point of laughing at him when he does this. He hates that.

Now then. Take yourself a wild guess at how Morris paid us back for not getting him a present and laughing at him. He ate Grandma's holy water. Oh yes. Chewed the be-Jasus out of the plastic can, turned it into a colander, and drenched my office with the stuff by shaking the can like a dead rat and spraying everything with the blessed H2o. Not much of a row when T.J. discovered that, then.

I have to say, that, co-incidence or not, my computer hasn't crashed since Morris anointed it with holy water. And the printer now only sucks in one sheet of paper at a time, rather than the scrunched-up ream that usually chokes it five times a day. Most spooky of all, the CD player on my mini hi-fi has picked up its bed and walked again, after two years of total inaction.

Tragically, Morris must have remained bone dry, despite the spiritual deluge he caused, because he's still the same stupid git-dog he's always been. And Grandma's divine request? Well, I was all for lobbing a tap-ful of Addlestone's finest in a Panda Pop bottle, mailing it to Donegal, and sending Herself off to confession to square it with Himself. Instead, my lot went and told Grandma the truth, including details of my perfectly acceptable plan. That wasn't very Christian, was it?

# From Our Inside-Broadcast Unit:

## Morris win the Sportsgit Of The Year award…

Aaaaaaand you join me at the Telzoffice Stadium, where the atmosphere is explosive and the appliances are nothing short of electric. As you can tell from the screams of Herself (the so-called 'home-supporter') Morris is enjoying a long-awaited return to the devastating form that made him a household name, and a celebrated insurance liability. After a worryingly poor run, a whole series of missed chances, and, amid rumours that calamity's golden child had lost his gift for pointless chaos, Morris has answered the sceptics in the finest way possible with a spectacular hat-trick.

Yes folks, the ultimate opportunist has struck three times in as many days, defying one of the most experienced defences in the Barkrealhard Premier League, Dopey Dogs Division. Morris's resurgence began with a superb solo effort, as, playing alone up front, he somehow latched onto a gallon of used frying oil and drank most of it before being tackled by Herself. Morris then set off on one of his hypnotic, swerving runs, leaving the home defence bewildered, before hitting the back of the net curtains with a perfectly-placed volley of projectile vomiting. Onlookers were stunned by the ease with which Morris strolled through the defenders and the post match analysis revealed that someone had played the container of oil on-side by leaving it and Morris umarked on the edge of his run. Payer-manager Terry Doe was disappointed, later reflecting "At this level, you can't drop your guard for a second. My lads' attention lapsed, Morris lapped, and we were all punished for it."

Within 24 hours the home team showed how little it had learned from the previous disaster, by allowing Morris to ghost in on the blind side and steal a tin of pilchards from an unattended shopping bag. Within the home turf of his bed, Morris set up a purposeful attack on the pilchards and penetrated their defence with his first real attempt. Coming in from the side, Morris continually exploited his favourite 'paw, paw, chew' formation, gradually wearing down the pilchard tin and draining its reserves by the minute. At full-time Morris's victory was complete, as a decisive head-shake scattered the pilchard remnants to the four walls of the Payer-Manager's office. Sadly, after this brief but absorbing tussle, Herself was at the centre of some angry scenes, eventually being sent off to a pretentious Surrey garden centre.

The bleach had barely dried, when, unbelievably Morris slipped his markers yet again. This time the touch of a true moronic genius was there for all to see. In fact, those present had to step over the results of it.

For his finale Morris had chosen the downstairs bathroom, and specifically the laundry basket as the medium through which his genius would be expressed. He began with a controlled display of distribution, mainly involving the emptying of the basket – an unfeasibly expensive, Ali Baba-style tribute to the designer wicker-persons' art – and the hiding of its riper contents for future extreme-sniffing sessions. Nothing remarkable here, until, with the basket empty, the decision was made to crawl into it. Being of a chunky body type, only the fore-portions of Morris could be squeezed into the neck of the basket but, once inserted, he was well and truly wedged.

Inside the basket, the spoonful of clotted mush that poses as Morris's brain soon sussed that being partially imprisoned in a wicker bottle wasn't the most fun a thick dog could have, and began withdrawal proceedings. This subtle tactic amounted to thrashing the trapped section of his fat frame from side to side, via the incredible power of his back legs, which were conveniently hanging outside the basket. Unbelievably, although his vision was limited to what he could see through the chinks in the wicker's weave, Morris managed to thrash his way out of the bathroom, through the kitchen and into the main dining room arena.

With sufficient space in which to display his ability, Morris couldn't be denied. Bucking and twisting like a rodeo stallion, Morris scythed down three chairs and a loitering vacuum cleaner within seconds. Then a particularly athletic thrash opened the spring-loaded glass door of the stereo cabinet, which was superbly torn from its hinges by the basket's return stroke. The sound of a house breaking always means 'Morris' to the opposition, and defenders converged from all directions. Even so, Morris managed one last show for the crowd by using the basket to backhand a hamlet of Herself's ornamental cottages from a low shelf, causing severe structural damage to the one with the thatched roof. Naturally, that was the most expensive and revered house'ette of them all.

Tragically, there were no cameras to record Morris's return to form, or even his post-display extraction from the laundry basket. This procedure took 20 minutes and eventually resulted in the deployment of some jaws-of-life secateurs to the neck of the basket to provide sufficient extraction width. Equally sadly, it seems there's no longer room in the modern game for true entertainers and Morris was sent to the sin bin for the rest of the day. The post-match investigation predictably concluded that the Payer-manager was entirely at fault for signing Morris in the first place and recklessly allowing him to bring his species, his breed and his owners into disrepute. An appeal has been lodged but the usual FA reaction is expected.

# To Smell And Back

## Morris is scent mad...

Hello world – it's Morris.

For Morris, stupidity's loyal crusader, it was a day like any other. He'd finally managed to pull both rubber tyres off the wheelie-bin but, sadly, he'd completely failed to swallow even one of them. True, those tyres would never again smooth the passage of the family trash can, so at least that was a bit of a result. That wheelie-bin had trundled its last Friday morning trundle. No longer would it emerge from Morris's bit at the side of the modest Addlestone three-bed-barely-detached to the front aspect, where the cable company had dug up (and consequently buggered-up) the pavement.

Morris hated that bin and had long cherished the notion of crippling it sufficiently to keep it in one place long enough to chew it into oblivion. Alas, unless those tauntingly chewable tyres could be crushed into un-repairable particles the morning's work would remain incomplete and Morris unfulfilled. Such a roller-coaster of emotions for a single, desperately thick, bull terrier to ride so early in the day. Triumph, achievement, endeavor and failure - and it was still pre-postman a.m.. Morris still had miles of time to improve on this day's potential.

Then 'she' walked by and her smell smacked Morris in the head harder than that playground swing had done when he was a puppy. Like the swing, her scent rendered him dazed and ever so slightly cross-eyed with the intensity of it all. Unlike the pain from the swing, this strange ache shifted immediately from his head, coursed through his body like the pulse from the electric fence he bit that time and settled firmly in the previously single-purpose facility which usually dangled between his belly and his bum. Olympic standard tingling followed immediately with scent-induced after-shocks pinging out mini-shudders as Morris's sexual sonar switched to full power.

"Hoooowwwwwwowwwwwllll", came the call of the wild, as Morris regressed from Canis Domesticus to a primeval guise of Humpus Vulgaris-Maximus. He hadn't a clue what was going on inside himself, only that some sashaying minx of a daschund had slipped him an airborne Mickey and he was under the influence of 100%-proof sex. Drunk in charge of a wafting, waggling, willy and totally incapable of driving it - or at least parking it in the bay nature had provided. Worse still, Morris couldn't even see the object of his overwhelming desire. All he had to go on was a smell. He could do nothing but howl his frustration and scrabble pathetically at the immovable wooden gate between himself and his carnal destiny, while his redundant doghood rattling along the gate slats like a stick against railings.

And then 'she' was gone, followed minutes later by the last remnants of her smell, which signaled the decline in Morris's raging desires, until finally he deflated - physically, mentally, spiritually and chemically. The last deflation stage, represented by a salvo of ghastly farts, quenched all trace of 'her' glorious scent from his world and caused Morris to retreat into his loveless kennel to sleep alone with his pointless willy.

Twenty minutes later 'she' came back, bringing her scent with her, only this time its intensity had increased to nuclear proportions. Even as Morris slumbered through his unrequited dreams the daschund's pheromones screamed out to his basic urges, commanding them to stir. Stir they did, too, as Morris's instantly re-flated willy all but catapulted him from his kennel and into howling, shuddering, gate-rattling action once more.

Still he had not seen the siren that caused such upheaval in his loins, yet he knew he must find her and do stuff...and things...and possibly more stuff, who knows? Morris didn't, certainly, but he was willing to go along for the ride - even if he didn't get one. Again, the tempest passed, leaving his emotions ragged and that untrained and impractical willy swinging uselessly in the very same breeze that teased him with 'her' scent.

The eye of the hormonal storm passed over and through Morris six times that first day and five the next, switching him on and off like an endearingly dim light bulb. After the third day, Morris was a spent force. Hollow-eyed, twitching of limb and pitiful to behold, he still danced the pheromone shuffle every time 'she' tippy-toed past the gate but she was always out of sight by the time his tireless willy dragged his worn-out body onto the dance floor.

# A Guide Dog For The Thick

Seeing his plight and commendably forgetting their lifelong war, Herself ushered him into the house. She soon ushered him out again, though, when a sly draught carried essence de seasonal daschund to Morris's nose and he began to howl his non-lover's lament and vigorously roger the pouffe.

From then, Morris served his time in my hermetically sealed, double-glazed and draught-excluded office, where no smells exist save the aroma of decaying final demands and a faint stench from a once bristling cactus, now imploding in shades of greeny-snot-yellow due to lack of everything required to keep a cactus healthy. Morris's passionate affair with a bitch's pong eventually petered out and his unique version of normality reigned once more.

'Never mind, Morris', I told him, sagely. 'Better to have sniffed and lost, than never to have sniffed at all.', old son. He'll get over it. Look, he's already chewing on the wheelie-bin. Bless.

# Down At The Old Bully And Bush

## Lavender blue, silly-silly...

When I first sat down to write this Morris piece, I had the subject neatly arranged and thoroughly researched. I was planning to ask the readership why several dozen of you have, during the past few years, requested that Morris be introduced to your own girly bull terriers, with a view to creating a wee posse of Morrisettes. It's a fair question, is it not?

Despite - indeed, because of - the traumas that Morris has so regularly put me through, there are people out there who wish to embrace my brand of misery by re-creating him. This intrigues and slightly spooks me, yet it's true. Sadly, I was unable to attend this year's Crufts, but the sturdy old sorts on the Dogs Today stand informed me that yet more would-be masochists requested details of Morris, with a view to committing Morris-breedage of the first degree. I say again, why on earth would anyone contemplate such a thing?

Do they intend to give a puppy to someone they loathe? Perhaps these folk are planning an insurance scam on their house and contents, using a Morris clone to destroy it from within so that they can claim new stuff? Or, perhaps the desirees of a Morris-hund have recently waved goodbye to their teenage children, and feel a parental need for something else that eats like a hippo, farts in company and trashes the house on a regular basis.

Anyway, my pre-write musings on the structure and form of this month's article were totally short-circuited when a glance into the garden showed Morris eating a lavender bush. Normally, when I catch him mid-scoff with something forbidden, I attempt to use the incident as aversion therapy. By arriving all displeased-like and scowling ferociously at him as I dispossess him of his latest chewy treat, I still cherish the idea that he'll connect my displeasure with the object he's crunching into oblivion and avoid a repeat. I am a fool for investing the slightest hope in this strategy but I cling to the idea that, one day, the penny may drop, albeit with a hollow and resounding 'splash'.

This time, I decided to allow Morris to graze upon the lavender bush until he exploded. I was alone in the house, so there was no chance of the children interfering with this groundbreaking experiment, and I was determined to see just how much of the bush that stupid bloody dog would devour. For those who don't own lavender bushes, allow me to describe one to you. At this time of year (mid March, we work ages ahead on this magazine) a lavender bush is little more than a herbaceous afro of dried twigs, last year's dead flowers and the odd greeny bit to show you that it's still vaguely alive and shouldn't be dug up. It is not remotely edible-looking. Even the usual list of garden plague-bugs won't go near it at this time of year. Yet, there was Morris scarfing down gobfulls of the stuff, and licking rapturously at any really woody stems he couldn't snip off and swallow.

I watched this madness for over 20 minutes, until I could stand it no longer and stormed into the garden to scowl at Morris in my usual ineffective manner. He responded to my snarl of 'Whaddayoudoin, you sod!' by snatching a last mouthful of lavender bush and slinking off back to his kennel to digest a bellyful of fragrant fronds. Meanwhile, I just stared at a bush with a dirty great lump out of one side, wondering what on earth had climbed into my dog's lame brain this time. I concluded that it was just another demonstration of the fact, that, the good Lord had installed another bowel where Morris's central nervous system should be.

Then, a few days later, I was writing one of my desperately witty speeches, while the boys took charge of the bar-b-que. From what I could see from my office, we were about to be treated to exploded sausages, gnarled black burgersh objects and chicken drumsticks so fire-hardened that they had definite hand-to-hand combat potential. The burgeresque offerings had been sacrificed over the coals in a fire-blackened tray, which now brimmed with semi-congealed fat and carbonised, meaty particles. How did my worthy sons empty this utensil? They grabbed it with a pair of tongs and tipped its slimy contents into the very lavender bush that Morris had been scoffing.

We'd had our first barbies of the year mere days before Morris had lunched on lavender salad. The mystery was solved. Rather than the lunatic browsing of a tasteless bush, Morris had been nibbling an anointed herb. It's tiny victories like this that keep me going, you know. And this one kept me going right up to the time the boys told me that they'd never, ever emptied the bar-b-que tray on that lavender bush before. Oh well, at least Morris's farts had a pot-pourri pong about them for a day or two. Tiny victories, folks - and getting tinier by the day.

# Pet Defectives

## Morris and George are on patrol…

Not a working brain cell between them.

It is my privilege to announce that, while he may rule unopposed the kingdom of the dense, Morris is not the only inhabitant of planet Duuh. My bull terrier has found a soul-mate. Although George the bulldog puppy has yet to lower his canine perception to within 10 fathoms of Morris's, he has the advantage of looking really thick, even when he isn't - yet.

This is on account of wee Georgie being bloody ugly. What? Oh howl me no howls of protest. I'll stand no hypo-criticism from fellow owners of pig-hideous hounds such as my own fair Morris. Don't tell me you chose that Boston terrier because they always manage to look so damn noble. Or that you spend hours gazing at your cherished pug, wondering why the hell he wasn't cast as James Bond instead of Pierce Brosnan.

No chaps. Us choosers of 'character' breeds chose them because we think they're marvellous. Everyone else on the other hand, thinks they escaped from God's reject bin. Never mind. Each to his own, that's what Morris and I say, don't we Morris? Morris says 'Yes'. Er…sort of.

So Morris is a pig, but George is one of those squished-up-face type pigs that look like what ordinary pigs would look like, if they did sumo wrestling or played professional darts. George is owned and worshipped like the Dali Lama, by my brother-in-law Christopher and his lovely wife Clare, who isn't an aggressive person at all, oh dear me no. The pair of them will be mortally wounded by my cruel attack on Georgie's handsomeness, but we all have to find out the truth some time.

*Dear Chris and Clare, George is taking liberties with the definition of 'ugly', OK? Thought you'd best know. Love, Terry.*

# A Guide Dog For The Thick

There, that's it sorted. Now on with this month's fascinating glimpse at life with Morris - and his wincingly attractive co-star, George.

These two have recently teamed up in the never-ending war against crime. Here before us stand Simple Sherlock and his multi-jowled sidekick, Columbo. Morris has the big Roman nose, so he's Holmes, and George, well he just looks like Columbo. More specifically, George looks like a pig-based Columbo who does sumo and darts.

Yet, our world is surely a safer place because of Morris and George, for they are the cutting edge of community policing. They are the neighbourhood watch dogs.

We patrol the streets before bedtime, each of us with our already alert brains set on 'Really, really, alert, actually', ever watchful for crimey things. To the casual observer, it's merely a couple of podgy blokes traipsing along behind two dogs that look like they were weaned too close to a source of radioactivity, but we know the truth of it, don't we boys? The boys are slobbering over each other a bit right now, but they do know, really they do.

Only the other night, three streets and a posh estate away from home, Morris stopped to sniff at something potentially very serious. George's razor-sharp sleuthing instincts somehow failed to notice that Morris had paused to carry out this essential sniffing, and George rammed him from behind, which completely ruined the investigation. Morris was on to something there as well, because I caught him looking clever for a second.

Our pig-ugly posse has had its successes though. In fact we've already thwarted an outbreak of gang warfare, and in the process prevented the looting, arson and mayhem that inevitably follows. We happened upon rival gangs of 10 year-olds, obviously hyped-up on the food colourings still found in exotic bubble gum and some of the more sinister sherbets. Fortunately, we arrived just as a 'roller blades are well-better than skateboards' row was about to turn into a major breach of the peace.

Obviously the sight of Morris and George waddling impressively toward the conflict, had even these seasoned criminals thinking twice about disrupting the community. Sure they tried to save face by pointing rudely at our brave lads and howling with laughter, but that old nonsense means little to such as we, who walk unafraid the mean streets of Addlestone.

It took one final confrontation between the gang leader and me, to quell the would-be riot, once and for all. 'I know your mother young lady, and don't you think I won't tell her. Now then.' I wagged my finger, Sherlock and Columbo wagged their tails - once again the metropolis breathed a sigh of relief.

# The Crawl Of The Wild

## Grub's up...and down...and...

Fans of Morris the Weetabix-brained bull terrier (and there are some, because they write letters to him - so there) will be jubilant to discover that this latest slice of his life actually ends with him as the hero of the piece. Sort of. A bit. 'Ish.

The scene was set for Morris's heroic act, when our three fine sons discovered fishing. Now don't go thinking that this is one of those 'noble dog defies a force-12 Nor' Easter to rescue stranded children from leaky dingy'- deals, OK? This is Morris were talking about.

No, fishing entered the family consciousness - and maggots entered our family home. Oh yes, those maggots. Great snap-lidded tubs of perfectly maggoty maggots. Multi-coloured, perpetually writhing, blowfly children, churning through themselves like portions of self-propelled pilau rice, reeking eerily of ammonia and destined to hula on a hook until some extremely coarse fish either snaps them up, or sucks them juiceless like a pomegranate pip.

Doing fishing involves carting things around in tubs, mainly reels, floats, swan-friendly weights and suchlike, so the to-ings and fro-ings of the boys' tub fleet masked the very existence of maggots for well over a month. But these things can't last and Herself finally sussed it as our eldest returned from a last-minute dash to the tackle shop, maggot-pot in hand.

While her dutiful son kicked his grubby trainers into the boot-bin, Herself flipped the lid of the temporarily unguarded maggot tub. Another lid-flip followed almost immediately, with me, maggots in general and the many me-based weird'isms of our children, as the main lyric of Herself's vocal blitzkrieg.

Morris took one look at Herself in lift-off mode and snuck out to my office, 'to hide beneath my desk and bravely pretend to be asleep. The children grabbed their rollerblades and were specks in the distance inside five seconds. Even the maggots probably dived to the bottom of their tub, leaving guess who to cop the flack?

I was accused of deliberate maggot-harbouring. 'You knew what your children were up to, and you just stood by and let me share my home with those disgusting creatures!', shrieked Herself. Bit over the top don't you think? Open your eyes woman. According to you, our entire life is based on you sharing your home with a disgusting creature. Some days it's Morris, some

No, it's not pilau rice
– although Morris
would have liked
second helpings.

days it's me. Ha, ha! I nearly said that, really I did. Instead, I frog-marched the maggots down to the shed and triple-bolted every door between us and them.

Herself snarled at us for a day or two, narrowed her eyes a lot and silently shook her martyred head whenever the subject of fishing cropped up, but seeing as we'd had her living cheek-by-jowl with pot-loads of crawling filth for the past month, I reckon we got off lightly. Then, the boys spilled two pints of maggots in the bedroom. Herself's bedroom. While she was in it.

None of my lot would own up to actually dropping the tub, but the maggots' presence was explained by the fact that the shed was too cold and our bedroom had the biggest radiator. Thus, one tub of maggots warming cosily, hidden behind Herself's dressing table was now manifested as wavelets of fleeing fly grubs that rippled across the lovingly tended pile of our bedroom carpet. This was the sacred floorcovering where the trainer of man had never set foot. Now its delicate roseblush hue was alive with a viciously uncoordinated splattering of yellow, red, bronze, and traditional deathly-white maggots.

Herself went whiter than the most deathly maggot in our moving carpet of larvae. No scream rent the air, just a trembling, squeaky bleat of 'Ohhhhh, nnnnnnno', which crept from a mouth now stuffed with her own fist. 'Yyyyyyyooooooo', trailed off into a one-vowel threat which meant that unless every single maggot was charmed from the carpet, the bedroom, the house and most of our native Surrey - we would be the next meal those maggots feasted upon.

Herself screeched off to her girly mate down the road, still wailing like a car alarm, as my lads and I sprang into action and manned the maggot pumps. Morris thought it was all a jolly game and helped enormously by pouncing on us every five seconds in his efforts to persuade us that wrestling with him was miles more important than maggot scooping. Morris was swiftly banged-up in my office.

After an hour of frenzied bulk-retrieval, followed by twenty minutes of hoovering the more athletic escapees from various crevices, and a brief but vigorous scouting party to pick off the stragglers, we'd re-captured almost the whole tub of maggots - but not quite all. The shortfall were sharing our home with us.

I now had to instruct my sons in the ancient Chinese art of 'Li-ying' before Herself returned. 'Now repeat after me children - there's not a single maggot left in our house Mummy, isn't that lovely?' Then I dared them to stray one syllable off this message and awaited Herself's return.

She came, she saw, she saw no maggots, we were spared. Obviously, even the temporary sharing of her home with a few million maggots meant that Herself required further counselling, so she grabbed a gallon of Liebfraumilch and returned to her mate's maggotless house. It was then that Morris shone like the hairy God he's so obviously always been.

Like the sharpest of drug-busting spaniels, Morris suddenly leaped to his feet, ears cocked, expression intent and those piggy eyes fixed - on a lone maggot making its way down the stairs. Then another was spotted, and slurped-up in simialar fashion as it broke from cover beneath the bedroom door. Our Morris was a red-hot maggot-wrangler, and he was right on the case.

That superb hound, that blessed pet, did a tireless seek and destroy job on no less than 46 maggots that evening, and remains on alert to this very day. Bless you Morris, you Meister Maggot-Hund you. It's just a pity Herself can't be told a single, solitary word about your priceless talent.

# Ground Farce

## Morris puts the 'dim' in 'Dimmock'…

A hanging basket….

Somewhere around 50 disasters ago I told you how we'd had our garden all designer'd-up. That project represents the greatest of my rare domestic successes and Herself has adopted our garden as her favourite child. When chaos reigns in the Doe des' res', as an unstoppable tide of teenage sons feud, fight and dispute ownership of scary cosmetic products, and washing piles vie with ironing piles in their race to the ceiling, and when I fail to prevent Morris being Morris, it's to the garden she retreats.

In 'her' garden, Herself can swap pandemonium for pansies, bedlam for buddleia and Morris for more glasses of medicinal wine. Herself simply raises a soothing patio parasol, flips her feet onto a teak-effect footstool and reclines her sun-lounger to exactly the attitude she prefers. If only the attitude of her family could be adjusted so easily, she sighs, as the inter-son wars rage unabated behind double-glazed patio doors.

The garden is Herself's sanctuary and we don't invade it when she's recovering from us. Morris is flat-out banned from it, whether Herself's retreating or not, on the grounds that he would turn structured serenity into a tank training ground inside an hour. I have no valid argument against this embargo. The fact is, Morris is on record as a consummate destroyer of gardens, mostly ours, and Herself keeps the photo-evidence handy as a reminder. I don't bother arguing Morris's case. Instead, I just live in fear of him invading Herself's retreat and rampaging, unsupervised, through its precious features. Guess what. It's happened.

Of course none of my sons left the patio door open. Definitely not. No way Dad. Not us Dad. Okaaay. Herself had gone shop-worshipping, so it must have been me then. Even though I wasn't in the house at the time, or in fact within 10 miles of it. Still must've been me, though, because all three of my normally scatterbrained sons have somehow developed perfect recall of their not leaving the patio door open and each has assured me that open door-leaving is something they'd not even contemplate, 'because we know Mum would go raving skitzoid'. Quite.

The fact is, the identity of the culprit matters not a jot. There's only one mug that's going to cop for this one and you don't need an 'ology to guess who that will be. Morris had been loose in the garden for less than 15 minutes, according to number two son who'd seen him asleep on his bed in my office when my son had absolutely-for-certain closed that patio door. During his romp in forbidden territory, Morris had concentrated his attention on the pretend Grecian urn water feature and had left Herself's beloved patio furniture completely unmolested. Apart from wee'ing on it all and doing an unfeasible amount of poos everywhere. So that was good, then.

The damage to the water feature was severe but not, I thought, beyond repair. The pretend urn had been skittled, but thanks to its traditional plastic construction it had failed to shatter. Restoring the urn to the vertical was the work of seconds and even re-threading its squirty water pipe didn't over tax my superb impression of Charlie Dimmock. The real problem was the electric cable that ran under the slabs.

....a hanging offence!

Morris had probably wanted to join the ants that scuttle freely beneath the equally fake 'stone' dish-thing upon which sits the squirting urn. This dish is filled with pebbles and acts as a sump for the water from which the feature gets its name. Anyway, the dish also houses the pump that powers the whole thing and from this runs the necessary cable. Or at least it did until Morris flipped the dish and ripped out the wiring. I don't do wiring. Worse still, Hurricane Herself could hit us at any time. While my sons went on an intensive garden poo hunt, I knew I needed a plan with lots of cunning in it. Failing this, I'd be forced to deploy the ancient Chinese art of li-ying. It is without a trace of shame that I went for the latter fixit.

I told Herself that the water feature had stopped watering and my mate the electrician reckoned there was a dodgy connection somewhere. He'd had a look, I said (which perfectly explained the disheveled appearance of the water feature) and he'd be back with a better terminal-interface- junction-box jobby as soon as he could. This gave me a few days to find and brief a handy mate and for once, I got away with my Herself avoidance scheme.

Then, while she was dusting the log pile, she noticed a monstrous poo and all hell broke loose. I made some feeble comment about it obviously being the former property of the scabby tabby that invades us but Herself was having none of it. 'It's a cat, not a sodding puma!' hissed Herself, using a degree of eye-contact on me that was, frankly, uncalled for. She was equally scathing about my suggestion that the 'dog log' could have been imported along with the tree-based versions among which it now lay. I knew there wasn't a chance that I could persuade any of my boys to take the rap for it, either, and this was one Morris fallout that I certainly wasn't about to own up to. So I shrugged a lot, looked mystified and said 'Dunno' at regular intervals.

Herself's not happy. Her sanctuary has been defiled and she's giving me and Morris the evil eye in equal measure. I'm breathing relief's very own sigh. I know what Morris can do to gardens and what could have happened if he'd done even some of it to ours. I'd have been without a water feature – in more ways than one.

# Playing God

## Shrine my patience...

Though Father Time's baby new year is still in nappies, 1998 has already emerged as my very own annus gloriatus. For I, Terry Doe, humble scribe of the parish of Addlestone, have become a god. Of course, this isn't my first time out as an object of worship. My children venerate me all over the place and I've lost count of the times Herself has looked at me and silently shaken her head in what is obviously pure adoration. Such is the life of the revered husband and father.

This deserved divine status of mine took an intense twist a few days ago when Morris decided that he'd spend the rest of his life as my follower-in-chief. Within hours of this decision, I became his reason to believe. Now everything he does, he does for me. Trouble is, like every notion with the tenacity to burrow itself into Morris's barely conscious consciousness, this one won't be denied. I am being adored to distraction. Morris and I have always been best of mates, and countless are the times I've rescued him from the wrath of Herself. My, how often we've taken to the hills together to allow the diffusing of yet another vow about taking the bread knife and turning Morris into a pyjama case. In return, Morris faithfully destroys every scrap of furniture in my study, eats the cables of my computer and scatters the slobbery, shredded contents of my wastepaper bin to the four winds.

At least, that's what he used to do. Now he collects and hordes holy relics that belong to me, his god. These go from all holy to all holey in a flurry of religious fervour, which manifests itself as Morris chewing the goodness knows what out of whatever it is he's knicked. Anything from a hanky to my orthopaedic mattress is likely to be dragged off to the grotto Morris has established beneath my office desk, and left there to be rolled upon and nibbled until all the essence of me has been absorbed.
Guess what Morris has chosen as his Holy Grail? My underpants. And he only goes for the unwashed ones. My discarded Y-fronts instantly become the sacred skiddies of Saint Tel the moment Morris hoiks them out of the laundry basket. The next thing I know, he's chomped through the crutch piece, and my bits find themselves hanging in a string bag like last year's Christmas brazils.

Morris drinks my bath water. He also sleeps with his nose rammed inside one of the rancid trainers I only ever wear when cleaning out the fishpond. These reeking Reeboks are forbidden entry into the shed, never mind the house, but Morris tracks them down and hides one in his grotto, sneaking it out and inhaling himself off to Nirvana after lights out.

# A Guide Dog For The Thick

When I read the paper, Morris has to sit on any part of me his bottom can reach. It's not the most pleasant of sensations to feel Morris's descending bum forcing his squidgy under portions between one's toes, believe me. You know that yogic flying lark? Morris can do that. There I am, peacefully ploughing through the usual acre of Sunday supplements when Morris materialises at my elbow for a scratch on the chin. Normal enough. Then, with no apparent effort, unseen and completely undetected, he's hauled his fat body onto my lap and I'm cuddling the hairy git instead of reading about some soap star who has turned her life around with ginseng and leeches.

Morris weighs about as much as a small family car, so how the hell does he drift about so spookily? Through religious worship of me. That's how. Doggie trick cyclists and Desmond Morris devotees will put my pet's dedication down to his place as subordinate in our family pack, with me as the dominant alpha male. That all applies perfectly if your pack happens to be mooching about the Serengeti plains looking for a gnu with a bit of a limp, or loping through the snowy wastes of North America on the trail of an elk. Here in Addlestone-On- Mud, that canine psycho-babble ain't worth diddly-squat-plop, mainly because the Alpha male in our pack happens to be a bitch... er, a female, that is. Nope, the truth is Morris has found his mission in life, and that mission is me.

Meanwhile, I'm running out of underpants and Herself thinks Morris has now become a weirdo, in addition to the cussed nuisance he's always been. Morris himself? Even as I write, he's sitting at his god's right hand. Actually, he's plonked his bum on my right foot   but it means the same to Morris.

# The Fool Monty

## Throwing in the towel...

"You just can't keep telling people how stupid that dog is, month after month."
"Er...yes I can actually, Dear. Because every month of his life, Morris comes up with brand new stupid stuff for me to write about. He's a vast resource of stuff-which-is-stupid - and some of us happen to find that stuff very entertaining."
" You didn't find Morris's latest episode 'very entertaining', though, did you?"
"Shaddup. That hurt my feet and I could've been locked up."
"Well? Are you going to tell them about it, or shall I?"
"Oh I'm bound to let you tell it, aren't I? You'd have me down as a pervy in the opening paragraph you would."
"So tell them then."
"Don't have to if I don't want to. S'my column, I'll write what I like."
At this point Herself started to lecture me about being childish, so to prove her wrong I stuck my fingers in my ears, closed my eyes and repeated "Lah,lah,lah,lah,lah,lah,lah,lah," as fast and as loud as I could until she went away. With the stage to myself, allow me to explain Morris's latest misdemeanour.

It started innocently enough, with me taking my Spring bath at 6 a.m. This early bathing deal is forced upon me by the bathroom blockade Herself and the kids set up once they awaken. I either hit the suds when the dawn chorus is still clearing its throat, or go to work smelly. Of course Morris won't be excluded from this ritual and plonks himself down the taps-end, gazing adoringly at me, his piggy eyes following my every soapy twitch.

Meanwhile, I prise the old season's grime from my body with a loofah the size of a sheep and generally sand-blast my recesses with industrial grade bath salts. I always know it's time to rise from the Radoxian ooze, when the surface crust is solid enough to support a mallard or two, and it was as this glorious spectacle was taking place that Morris made his move.

Quite simply, he knicked my dressing gown off the towel rail and buggered off out the back door with it. Except it wasn't quite that simple, because thanks to Morris having already chewed up the dressing gown the kids gave me for Christmas, the one he was currently dragging around the garden was the only one I've got.

I'm lost without my dressing gown. I need it to throw about me when I scramble downstairs to stop Morris barking at the central-heating timer - (don't ask). It's that gown I reach for when I wake in the night and my tuned nostrils detect Stench De Maurice, above the creeping whiff of Herself's essential oil burners.

# Grief Encounters

## A weird woman and new friends ahoy...

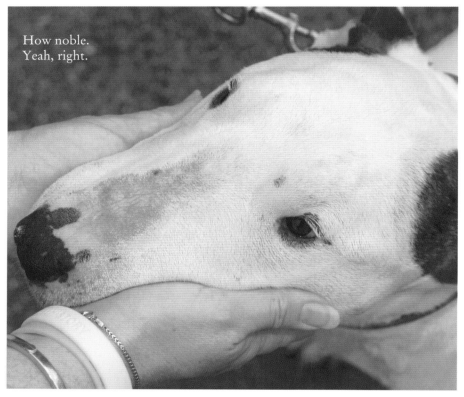

How noble.
Yeah, right.

"Oh, isn't he LOVELY!" gushed the slightly scary, 40-something lady with the floating purple dress, henna graffiti on her feet and twisty-rope hair. "What's his name? He is a boy isn't he?" She glances boldly at Morris's bits shining pinkly in the flattering glow of a Surrey evening sun, before re-gushing, "Oh yes he CERTAINLY IS, isn't he?!" Some people have no shame.

I told her that his name was Morris, although it often gets abbreviated to 'Thatbloodyflea-bag' or 'Yoursoddingdog', according to his disaster rating at the time, ha-ha. Now kneeling in front of Morris and ignoring me completely, she cupped his empty head in her also-henna'd hands. With her face so close to his that I could see the reflection of her silver nose-piercings in my dog's piggy eyes, she said breathily, "He should be called Thor. That's what I'd call him if I was his friend. Yes, Thor. Or possibly... Alice."

"Alice?" I squeaked, having accepted 'Thor' as suitably noble and godly for one such as Morris.

"Yeah. As in Alice Cooper, y'know?"

"Oh right." I replied, as though the connection between a mega-dense bull terrier and a '70's rocker who did strange things with snakes and guillotines was as natural as her body odour.

I'm not very good with weird women, despite the fact that both Morris and I seem to attract our unfair share of them. Flaky females tend to put me on the back foot, due I suspect to their unerring ability to become loud, eccentric or theatrical all over the place, and all the more so in public, where my natural shyness is at its most intense. I wanted out of this encounter before the middle-aged moonchild started scattering crystals or claimed some ancient right to urinate in the street.

Thankfully, she must have had a heavy date with a druid or something, because she rose to her decorated feet, threw us a "Gottago" and skip-floated toward the nearest pub in an exaggerated cloud of purple with henna scribbles. Watching her drift away, her mousey hair-ropes swishing in time to the carefree swing of her many-bangled arms, I found myself smiling at our encounter and searching for a one-line description of that remarkable woman. I settled for 'mad old hippy'.

She is just one of many 'colourful' characters Morris and I stumble across during our various mooches around Surrey, and she's by no means the most bonkers. That title surely belongs to the owner of an impressive gin ranch of a boat, who, catching sight of me and Morris waddling through the Thameside rain one morning, bid us take shelter on his craft. To this day I can't imagine why I responded to this strange man's bellow of "Come aboard, man!" and wild beckoning toward the awning of his ship-ette. He could have been a maritime mad axeman for all I knew. Yet, within seconds of that hollered invitation, Morris and I were squelching up the boat's gangplank-thingy and I was sniffing suspiciously at a treble gin and tonic, with (I kid you not) frozen pink elephants floating in it.

The elephants were gel-filled, plastic, re-freezable examples of middle-class humour. Much the same could be said about mine floating host, actually, and all could certainly be applied to his wife. Now here's the really embarrassing bit. You know I said that Morris and I were invited aboard via loud vocals and lavish beckoning? Well, it turned out that the boat owner wasn't calling and waving to us at all but to an acquaintance of his a hundred yards away. Eeek! I discovered this fact around two hours and five monstrous G&Ts into my first meeting with 'Mac', as he called himself, and 'Joycie' as he called his wife between orders for more drinks.

Morris took it all in his stride, of course, and after widdling on something chrome with a neatly coiled rope attached, simply crashed out on deck for a rainbathe. To be fair, while she was sober and awake, Joycie loved Morris and cuddled him frequently whilst blocking his arteries with vol-au-vents and other designer tidbits. But when all's said and done, how mad must anyone be to allow a sodden, shambling hulk and his equally damp dog to stomp uninvited onto your holiday home? Mac showed not a sign of surprise that a huge quantity of strange man and odd dog had just boarded his boat. Instead, he broke out the Gordons and we became instant drinky-mates.

Sadly, Mac and Joycie were mere weeks away from permanently exiling themselves in Florida – he told me the reason for this transplant about six drinks in, but I've gin and gone and forgotten it – and my first meeting with the couple was also my last. We've swapped e-mails and the invitation to stay with them in Florida is repeated every time, but I'm hesitant to say the least. It took me two full days to recover from that brief, unexpected gin-fest (I never drink gin) so it's fairly obvious that long-term exposure could be fatal.

As I said, during our bonding-walks, Morris and I have met a ripe old allocation of eccentrics, unique personas, one-offs and downright nutters. The real point is – I wonder how many of them say the same thing about us?

# Wanted – Bull Terrier?

## Be careful what you wish for...

I am still being informed that my accounts of life with Morris and his jolly japes prompt desires to own a bull terrier. Not just a bull terrier, you understand, but one every bit as bonkers as Morris. As ever, this truly astounds me. When I first read Moby Dick, I was awed, impressed and captivated by Herman Melville's epic, but it did not, for one instant, inspire me to pick up a harpoon and jump the first whaler out of Surrey. Yet, even as I stack disaster upon calamity before this readership, there will be those who regard the whole teetering pile of Morris-based mayhem as his finest recommendation.

It is no such thing. It is a sworn statement from someone who loves his dog despite these catastrophes, not because of them. Geddit? It's a sad fact that, possibly as early in the relationship as his 50th major disaster, many would-be bull terrier owners certainly wouldn't be bull terrier owners any longer. At least they wouldn't be the owners of the one called Morris. He takes some sticking, does my dog.

I, of course, have no choice but to laugh in the face of adversity, and cry when I'm cowering in the shed, at night, with the lights off, hiding from Herself because Morris has taken the stairs carpet up for the third time in a week. Whereas you, dear, unsuspecting desirer of a dopey dog, still have the chance to choose a normal one. I say grasp that chance. Grasp it as Ahab's shipwrecked crew grasped the upturned hull of their lifeboat, and spare a thought for me, your Captain, forever lashed to a lumbering white monstrosity that lays waste to all before it. You don't suppose that I'm over-doing the melodrama a tad, here, do you?

It has to be said, though, Morris is more than ever-so-slightly not your average dog. For once, I'm not bleating on about his mollusc'ian mental agility. It's his sheer physicality which sets his breed, and him specifically, apart from normal canines. Morris is a cod-headed, barrel-chested, pink-testicled bull terrier, and he definitely requires specialist handling.

He's ideal for me, of course, but then I'm undeniably 6-foot 4 and a gazillion stones of impressive heft. I can usually steer Morris fairly reliably and rarely crash him during walks in built-up areas. This is important. A badly-driven Morris could be a serious hazard among pedestrians and only those with the ability to coax along the canine equivalent of an HGV should apply for this particular dog licence.

Morris once collided with someone who was waving a collection tin outside Tescos. At no more than a determined waddle, Morris's head hit the collector in the side of the knee and dropped him like one of Fred Dibnah's chimneys. I can still hear the death-rattle of the collection tin as it rolled along Tesco's forecourt. I could have been sued and the unfortunate collector was almost a write-off. All because I momentarily fell asleep at the lead. I say again, these are not ordinary dogs.

In telling you lot these facts of my bull terrier's life, I'm undoubtedly preaching to the converted. Dogs Today readers are a seriously clued-up cluster of humanity. From my readership communications over the years, it's obvious that I've nothing to teach the DT stalwarts. However, there are a few whose warts aren't quite so stal', and it is to these good folk I direct my sermon.

Thou shalt not...no, that's a tad too sermonly. Look, what I'm so clumsily trying to say is, as much as you think you want a dog just like Morris, you can't think about getting even a normal bully until you've passed what I refer to as the suitabullyty test. All I ask is that ye be true unto thine own selves. Now you've made me come over all biblical. I hope you're happy.

Righty-ho. Why do you want a bull terrier, then? Go on, be honest, and if the word 'macho' ever drifts through your mind, then you've already failed the audition. Too many dogs act as egos-on-leads, to too many inadequate owners. If you want to look hard, go to the gym and pump something. If you're too lazy to do that, then you're too lazy to own a bull terrier. Dogs Today readers aren't sad, pseudo-macho types, so that mini-rant probably hammered home with the force of a warm marshmallow plopping onto a duvet. Never mind, it always does me good, and that's why I write this stuff, after all.

For the record, I began by loving the shape of the bull terrier, after which I fell for their affection, loyalty, tolerance, sense of fun, and half-a-dozen other qualities that I can't recall right now, possibly due to their being overtaken by Morris's disgraceful conduct over the years. I still love the shape of them, too. I think they're physically perfect, actually. Perfect for me, that is, whose own shape has drifted over the years and now sadly leans more toward 'walrus' than anything else.

All I'm trying to tell you is that a pseudo-Morris isn't the dog for you, ok? Trust me on this, I'm the world authority on this subject. Been there, seen the film, read the book, got the T-shirt – Morris ate the T-shirt and the book, end of story. Now, you divert your search for a canine friend to pastures normal, and let the sole occupant of Morris-Purgatory finish his sentence in what passes for peace around here. You know it makes sense.

# Old Dog - New Tricks!

## In which I lower Morris's achievement crossbar below ground level...

The guilty look that Morris has made his own.

You'll never believe what I'm going to tell you. You won't, you know, because what I'm going to tell you is, frankly, unbelievable. But it's true, so believe it, ok? Right, here goes; I've taught Morris some tricks! Yes I blimmin'-well have, so don't scoff like that. Morris, previously the most impervious dog in living memory, has absorbed not one, but three tricks in slightly less time than it takes to train a dead jellyfish.

I did it for a bet. Herself had watched a friend's collie go through its routine of party pieces – which finished with this swatty-geek pooch making a soufflé rise or something – and I was harangued about how useless Morris is for a solid week afterwards. I bet Herself that I could teach our old dog per-lenty of new tricks, and she went and took me up on it. I was a victim of my own delusion for a while, but I adapted and overcame and now Morris can do tricks.

His first two tricks are seriously impressive, actually. He has to do both tricks at the same time, but they really are amazing to watch. Morris not only catches something I throw to him, he sneezes on command. Come on, you've got to admit that's impressive. It works every time, too. All I have to do is stand about a foot away from him with a violently-shaken can of Diet Coke (Morris and I are counting the calories at the moment, see?) then I repeatedly lob it toward his empty head until he manages to catch it. Morris immediately scrunches the can, Diet Coke sprays everywhere and this makes him sneeze. This is mainly a trick to do outdoors, but trust me, it looks even slicker than it sounds.

I know you're going to find this next statement a bit hard to accept, but Morris's latest piece of performance art is even more applause-worthy than his catch 'n' sneeze trick. Oh yes, we've really pushed back the frontiers of humano-canine interaction on this one. So far, we've only once perfected the routine I'm about to describe, but I have every confidence that we'll soon have it sorted on a regular basis, and then I'll set up evening classes and teach you lot how to do it. So there's that to look forward to at least.

Picture the scene if you will. In fact you have to picture the scene because this is a magazine not the telly, so you haven't much choice really. Anyway, there we are Morris and I, out taking the early morning air on a seemingly deserted piece of Thames bankside, when Morris decided that he was bored with being a dog and wanted to try being a fish.

For no reason I can think of, Morris abused his off-leash status and leapt like some pink-testicled Moby Dickhead, straight into the Thames. This was very much the early spring and Father Thames was still winter-swollen and extremely grumpy. Morris's flirtation with fish-hood ended as soon as his fat body hit the brown, swirling water. He wanted out, and sharpish. The river, however, had other ideas. It wanted to take Morris for a joyride and Morris didn't have the sense to turn tail and strike out for the shore.

Instead, he went into torpedo mode and paddled furiously with the current until he was cresting along at roughly the speed of the Isle Of Wight ferry. Here's where we learned our latest trick. Now, what I'd like to tell you is, when I made a noose from Morris's flexi-lead and attempted to lasso him as he torpedoed past, he caught the noose in his clever gob and allowed me to haul him ashore. Sadly, what really happened was Morris continued to paddle like a thick dog possessed until he collided with a reed bed and became lodged about five feet from the bank.

There then followed an unbelievably tedious 20 minutes of me begging Morris to 'at least soddin' TRY to get out, you hairy git!', followed by millions of failed lassoing attempts. I managed to get the noose over his head loads of times but he just shook it off and lay in the mud from which the reeds were growing. Morris was the least intelligent living thing in that reed bed, of that there is no doubt.

I was resigned to a stimulating wading session, when one of Morris's walkies mates turned up attached to Jerry-The-Reasonable-Plumber, who is so-called because he is. When Morris saw Jerry-The-Reasonable-Plumber's dog, he simply walked out of the reedbed, shook a gallon of Thames mud over me, and trotted off with his mate to find cowpats to roll in.

Do you know, to this very day, whenever Morris and I are walking along the Thames, all I have to say is, "Morris, DON'T jump in the river" – and he doesn't! Amazing trick, or what?

# Escape Claws

## And nail...the end is near...

Should you have noticed a distinct lack of crack troops, S.W.A.T. teams and Special Forces agents in your area of late, the reason is simple - they're all being combat trained in the art of clipping Morris's toenails. Morris absolutely hates having this done and howls like a tart as soon as he sees the clippers, inevitably ending up rampaging round the house trailing whichever volunteer has been foolish enough to hang on to his leg. He's ten times as bad if I let the vet do it, so I don't. Consequently, my family has come to dread the task even more than Morris does.

Dread or no dread, like tax forms, Christmas and school holidays, 'that bloody job' always comes around again, and with it the moans, groans, excuses not to attend the ritual and all of the other predictions of disaster that go with clipping a few horny millimetres off dear old Morris. I always know when it's time to alert the family that clippin' time approacheth, when Morris gets a claw or two entangled in my dressing gown during his compulsory 20 minute rearing-up session as I let him out for a widdle in the morning.

Sure enough, this very a.m., as I waddled foggily downstairs to open Morris's sluice gates, his front paws raked my towelling wrapped midriff and pulled yet another snag from what is no longer a dressing gown at all really. My fearful diagnosis was confirmed by a distinct 'click' from Morris's front offside paw as he padded across the quarry tiled floor of my office. Sure enough, there was the culprit, curling from his foot like a particularly attractive piece of pork scratching. As nominal head of the household, it fell to me to make the announcement. "Gather about me family - it's clippin' time and no mistake."

Ever the optimist, before casting my family into the pits of despair I went for the miracle option and had a go at snipping Morris single-handed. I set up a decoy move, by planting myself at the computer in a perfect imitation of someone replying to a very flattering piece of fan mail from a nice lady called Janis. The nail clippers were at my right hand while I tapped out my reply to the kindly Janis, and Morris responded to my hearty slap on my thigh by rearing up to see me, his front paws dangling forgotten and well within clipper range.

Diverting his attention with an ear-scratch, I snuck the clippers into position, their mechanical jaws set to remove a quarter of an inch of curly toenail at the next squeeze of my hand. At least that was the plan.

Soon as he felt the slightest pressure on his claw, the game was up. Morris let out a howl that all the lost souls in hell couldn't match, pulled his defiled foot from my grasp and made a dash for the back garden - straight into the glass of the patio doors. How these held I'll never know, but Morris bounced off them and headed for the hills, or in his case the stairs.

Battering open our bedroom door with his head, Morris leapt upon Herself as she slept, which produced another howl of almost the same intensity as Morris's. From the bed to the dresser cannoned Morris, trashing Herself's teddy bear collection and scattering her treasured flock of porcelain geese like a marauding fox. By now, my noble gesture of not disturbing the family with the toenail clipping job, had been somewhat compromised.

With me blocking his escape through the door, Morris turned his attention back to the bed and that protesting lump under the duvet. Herself, who not 10 seconds previously, had probably been dreaming of unlimited credit card thrashing in New York, now found her cosy cocoon being burrowed into by a hyper active hound with curly toenails. This was not a recipe for a happy morning.

As Morris insinuated himself into one end of the duvet, Herself was squeezed toothpaste-like, from the other, her face contorted into that familiar, 'are you ever going to cop it for this' expression. No time to placate she-devils for me, I had me some serious clippin' to do.

Hastening my three fine sons to my side, I bid them flop onto the writhing mound of duveted Morris and pin him down. Then, by fishing around under the covers and pulling out anything of Morris's that contained toenails, I had him clipped and sorted in no time. Sure, the occasional son was catapulted to the ceiling by Morris's attempts to escape and one of Herself's china geese now sports a Superglued neck, but compared to the war wounds usually suffered by my house and its occupants, this clippin' time was a breeze.

So, all I've got to do now is lob Herself out of bed whenever Morris needs a manicure. Although, come to think of it, having to handle one uncooperative creature that costs me a fortune is hard enough as it is - without upsetting Morris as well.

# Pen-Pal (Not)

## His nibs munches my Mont Blancs...

Morris immortalised.

Everyone knows that whenever Morris does one of his drastics I make excuses for him. I will also invent alibis for him, flat-out lie for him and, if all else fails and I can't blame my children, I'll even take responsibility for him. Well, not this time, I won't. This time, Morris has struck me a mortal blow.

A blow so bad, so deeply wounding and so monumentally upsetting, that it will be weeks before I'm able to look into Morris's piggy eyes without snarling at him. Me and Morris ain't mates no more. I'm not speaking to him and I don't care if he ever plonks his scabby chops on my knee ever again...ever. And even if he does, I'm not doing the scratch-me-at-the-bottom-of-my-ears number. We're finished. He's done the one thing I can't forgive him for. He's chewed up my matching set of Mont Blanc pens. To be precise, he mangled two pens a propelling pencil and the presentation case. The evil, spiteful, rotten, farty, git.

I loved those pens. No, really, I genuinely adored them, and I'm the least materialistic human on this earth. As far as being materialistic goes, I make Ghandi look like Ivana Trump, yet those precious, blessed, divine conveyors of the written word had me totally in their thrall. I was all thralled-up over those Mont Blancs. It was love at first write and we were an item from the day my father-in-law gave them to me.

Wherever I went, my Mont Blancs went with me. I signed my mortgage papers with the fountain pen, I wrote out our first child's first birthday card (including a desperately funny poem which he completely failed to appreciate) with the rollerball and I once defended my entire family from a kamikaze bumble-bee, using only my courage and that now deceased propelling pencil. Will my life ever be the same again? I think not.

Herself discovered the tragedy when she was hauling out Morris's stash of stolen goodies from his cave beneath the posh desk in my office. This is Morris's grotto, where he hordes anything he can swipe that smells of me. The magnitude of what Herself saw lying among the usual nest of my socks, underpants and bits of dental floss stirred even her grating block of heart-substitute granite. For the first time in her entire career as Morris's mortal enemy, Herself tried to defend him.

She knew better than to diminish the seriousness of what Morris had done to my Mont Blancs. He'd climbed onto my posh desk, rootled through my open briefcase, extracted my sacred presentation case and retired to his grotto to obliterate my pen set at his leisure. After all we've been through together those pens positively reek of me and must have been irresistible to Morris's whiffly hooter. They certainly didn't put up much resistance to his teeth and by the time I was allowed to view the remains, my cherished pens resembled something sketched by Dali, when he was seriously pissed.

So, that's my Mont Blancs gone, then. No more flourishing them at meetings. No more snapping shut the lid of their cool case to attract the attention of those forced to pilot Parkers or scratch about with a Sheaffer, or, heaven forbid, blob-up big style with a Bic. I've Monted my last Blanc, and there's no way back. They're gone. He's eaten them. He's pooed them. They've been bagged, binned and burned. I think I'm going to cry now.

I'll remember the good times, of course. When that lout from the advertising department accused my Mont Blancs of being counterfeit and dared compare them to a monstrous set of fakes he'd dredged from some shifty street trader in New York. My pens and I soon sorted him out, and we exposed his dodgy Rolex while we were about it, too. How about that time when they were openly admired by Darth Vader, then? Oh yes. Darth, well it was Dave Prowse who played him, actually, said that my pens were 'very nice', when I interviewed him once. I didn't prompt him or anything, he just said it. Dave was also the Green Cross Code bloke, and he's been in loads of films and does tons of autographs, so he's bound to know a good pen when he sees one, and he was looking at three of them when he gazed so admiringly upon my Mont Blancs. Bless. Now I'm definitely crying.

Morris knows that I'm upset. Thick he may be, but he reads body-language like Herself reads my credit card receipts - instantly and with unfailing accuracy. He knows alright. I know he knows, because he hasn't done a single drastic since he murdered my Mont Blancs. Herself's trying to persuade me that the sacrifice of my pen friends may be worth it, if Morris continues to behave himself. I say no, no and thrice no. That's a 'no' for each of my ex-pens. Then, I look hurt and bereaved and go to the garden, where I can stare wistfully and Herself can see me doing it and feel sorry for me. I think it's only proper.

I'd better go now. This subject is even closer to my heart than I realised and my shining eyes and snotty nose are in need of a hanky - which I don't have because Morris has knicked them all and dragged them off to his grotto, where my Mont Blancs met their maker. I'm very, very, sad. But I guess you knew that already.

# Stains On My Character

Morris gets creative with creosote...

Powerful painkillers were my pre-show cocktails.

Among the global traumas flung at us daily by our TV screens, my own, 'How the hell do you get creosote out of a white dog', has to rank fairly low. Even Vanessa Feltz has more problems than I have right now, which is a huge source of comfort to me, as you can imagine.

Morris's head is still mostly creosote-coloured, though, and with but a few days to go before I parade him publicly at the Bull Terrier Club Welfare 'do', I'm an even-more-worried-than-usual man. Of course I knew, beyond any shadow of every doubt, that Morris would throw me a major wobbly before the event. It's the rules - always has been, always will be. I fully expected him to dislocate a tail or two in the run-up to our big day, or at least eat an item of occasional furniture and regurgitate Dralon and tassels all over any visiting bull terrier-type dignitaries. But, because he's sooooo funny and convenient to own, the little chap came up with a far jollier wheeze than I'd anticipated. He went and had a kip in a puddle of creosote.

# A Guide Dog For The Thick

I recklessly provided the creosote, via anointing a trellis with some and yes, it was me that left the brush within range of my dopey-crutch dog. The brush was soaking in a pot of white spirit. On my workbench. In my shed. Where real-world brushes should be safely soaking. Madly, I failed to triple dead-bolt the shed door and surround it with electrified razor wire, and Morris hoiked out the creosote brush, carted it off to his kennel and used it as a pillow. Super.

Thinned by the spirit, that creosote crept superbly into the pile of Morris's fur, thus creating a patch of diarrhoea-coloured stain on the large head which houses his tiny brain. Now my dog has a poo-tinted head. Rather, half of his head carries number-twos' highlights, the other half is traditional bull terrier brindle. Had Morris plonked his brindle bit on the creosote brush, I could have blended in the stain with a dab of creative creosoting here and there. As it is, I'm faced with ramming  Morris in Herself's Hotpoint on 'Non-Fast Coloureds - Heavy Soil', or creosoting him completely.

It's not only his useless head that's creosoted, you know. Ever tried getting that stuff off toenails? Well I have, and it doesn't happen. Because it didn't taste very nice, Morris tried to rend my creosote brush using paw-power alone. This squidged creosote, cuticle deep, into his every front claw and as Morris is a total poof about having his nails touched, there's no way I can scrub them clean. So, whatever tint his head assumes, Morris will make his public debut with dump-brown nails. Won't that look nice. No, it'll look stupid, and entirely fitting, given what those toenails are growing out of. Maybe I'll leave him in his muck-stained state and insist that he's the first of the soon-to-be desperately fashionable line of Addlestone Krapp-Hunds.

Creosote apart, there is another teensy problemette to be dealt with before Morris and I bathe 'neath the spotlight of Bull Terrier Club fame. You see, as I write it's Friday. Traditionally, Friday comes a mere two days before Sunday, which is when the much feared 'big day' dawns. The problem I have, and don't take this the wrong way, is that it's 48 hours before showtime, and I'm stoned out of my brains on heroin. Ok, Ok, so it's not heroin, it's morphine, prescribed by my surgeon for when my back goes walkabout, but trust me, Houston, we do have a problem.

I daren't tell Juliet Shaw, the show organiser, that I spent most of yesterday writhing about in hospital, because she's already phoned in dire panic after dreaming that Morris and I had left the country. If a mere dream had Juliet in that state, just imagine what a carefully couched "Oh hello Jules, just thought I'd mention that me bleedin' spine's snapped again, Ok?", sort of call could do. Nope, can't think about telling her to lay on a paramedic team, "just in case, like", or she'll freak for sure. By the way, you can dismiss any notions of me being a brave wee soldier, here. Basically, I'm terrified of Juliet Shaw and would rather risk spinal surgery with a rusty tin-opener, than even slightly annoy her.

Gosh, I'm still a trooper, though, aren't I? Please say I am, because Herself prefers a less complimentary description. Herself also reckons that Morris has been waiting for this opportunity for ages and the stage is set for him to get his own back on me for revealing all of his misdemeanors. She predicts that Morris will cock his leg against the poshest person there, that he'll up-chuck into at least one picnic basket and that he will, without a doubt, head-butt half-a-dozen show-goers who chuckle him under the chin. The crowning moment will be when Morris tows my limply protesting body around the show ring for several circuits, while I cling to his lead in a back-spasm. Cheerful old sort, my missus.

Anyway, by the time you read this, it'll all be over and once again, Vanessa Feltz will have far more things to fret about than I do. Unless Morris lives up to Herself's prediction of course, whereupon I'll make Juliet Shaw's dream come true and bravely leave the country. Pass the morphine, dear.

# Show(Up)Time!

## What the hell have I volunteered for?...

You know when you agree to do something, and even as you're saying 'Ho yes, I'll do that, I certainly will, no problem at all', you really want to bite your stupid fat tongue off? Well, I've just done that. Now I'm right in it and I know I'm going to make a complete and total wossname of myself. Naturally, it's all down to Morris.

Obviously, if I'd never shared my house with a dopey bull terrier like Morris, then I would never have been moved to write about him, and nobody would know who we were, so there's no way we'd have been invited to appear at a Bull Terrier Welfare fundraising event and I wouldn't be frightened to death. Which I now am, for loads of terrifyingly valid reasons. Most of these reasons are currently lying across my feet, snoring like a chainsaw and liberating anal wafts that are slaying houseplants two rooms away.

A proper bull terrier event, though. One of their major fund-raisers and bound to be full to bursting with proper bull terriers and proper bull terrier people. Eeeek. What'll they think of Morris and me? I bet their dogs haven't got permanently scabby noses, because they're stupid enough to keep poking them through the bars of the gate for next-door's cat to swipe at. And not a one of those posh dogs will have a single, over-long toenail on their nearside-left foot, because their owners were just too bloody knackered to cut it, after thrashing around on the floor for two hours to get the other fifteen snipped off.

Have a guess how many of the supermodel bullys on display at these events, will sport a self-chewed leg? None. That's exactly how many. Morris was attacked by the first gnat of the year, and he's relieved the itch by gnawing his own leg until it's gone damn near hairless and pink. Lovely. Won't that look professional amid those packs of the perfectly formed and graciously groomed? Oh gawd, why did I say I'd do this?

What about me, though? I'm in a worse bloody state than Morris. I'm even fatter than he is these days and my coat's falling out in handfuls. Nothing else for it, we'll be needing a makeover, Mo' 'n me. More like a miracle-over, judging by the multi-jowled reflection that my bathroom mirror insists on producing every morning. Must get a better mirror.

Seeking reassurance, I phoned the fiendishly friendly Juliet Shaw, who's one of this magazine's breed advisors and the person most responsible for inviting me into this mess in the first place. I was desperately hoping that Juliet would play the whole thing down a bit, and tell me that this event was no big deal, really, nothing much at all. More like a wee happy picnic, with a dog or two tacked on.

Some chance. Juliet cheerily informed me that 'Simply loads of people are waiting to meet Morris, and they can't wait to see what he looks like in the flesh.' Er... he looks like a scabby white pig that was designed by a committee. With one long toenail and a bald leg. And he's miles more attractive than I am, by the way. Now what?

Training, that's what. Training, and grooming and clipping and ...and...praying. Yes, tons and tons of praying. Any old God will do, in fact I'll have a bash at them all, just so's I don't miss the one who's in charge of making good impressions at fundraising dog-type events. I may even start chanting, or wandering around in orange chiffon, banging on a tambourine. That should get Morris's attention, not to mention Herself's. Oh yes, I've told Herself about my star appearance. She was about as calming as Juliet Shaw, she was. 'I hope they're not expecting too much.' Said my wife, hugely forgetting that she's the woman who's been employed to adore me these past fifteen years. 'I bet all the other dogs are real show-stoppers as well.'

Oh great. Just brill. Like fanx a bunch, wifey. Remind me to be that honest the next time you ask me if your bum 'looks fat in this dress'.

Right then, no time to lose. I'm scribbling a dirty great red ring around July the 18th., D-Day. 'D' for 'Dog show', not Disaster, Dire, Disown, or, in the words of the great Homer himself, Doh!

Morris and I are now officially in training. We'll be a joggin' and a workin' out, with towelling headbands, pink shellsuits and wired for sound with our personal sterios blasting 'Born To Run' into our sweaty earholes as mile after mile of fitness is absorbed and thoroughly enjoyed. Or... we might just say, 'Sod this for a lark' and come as we are.

Whatever happens, we'll be there on the day and we'll need your support. So, if you've got a spare one - bring it with you. To save you looking for us, I'll be the one with the red face who's attached to the scabby-nosed mutt with a sticky-out toenail and a baldy leg. Help!

# Fame 'N' Shame

I'm humiliated in public…again…

Morris and his
Morrisabilia

You know how some things can turn out to be a bit of a let-down? When predictions aren't quite fulfilled and the keen edge of anticipation is dulled by boring reality? Well that's exactly what didn't happen when Morris and I attended the annual Bull Terrier Club fund raiser at White Waltham. No let-downs there, folks. Not a one. Morris performed like a trooper. Ask the entire audience.

As explained in last month's column, I very nearly didn't make the show, due to my having wrenched my spine. I'd cleverly attempted to lift 80lbs. of wet Morris from a passing river, and something went 'karunchity-pop', in a place that shouldn't make that sort of noise at all. Anyway, I was spinally done-for and could remain upright only by the good grace of morphine and anything I could prop myself upon. But I was terrified of Juliet Shaw, the show organisor, so with eldest son, Kristopher, as a human zimmer frame, I made it to the show as promised. Bless me and save me.

Morris didn't look too bad, by his standards at least, and the creosote he'd smothered himself in a few days before was but a triple-scrubbed, yellow smudge on one side of his empty head. Juliet met and greeted us and asked us to wait while we were announced to the waiting crowd. A couple of Morris stories had been published in the excellent Bull Terrier Club magazine, so most of the crowd already knew what a total disaster he is. Then, after a fine intro by the nice man on the microphone, Morris and I strode into the spotlight of the main show ring. Fame at last.

We were met by warm applause, as I, smiling my best morphine smile, prepared to say a few well-chosen words. No need for words. The warm applause changed instantly into gales of cackling laughter, as Morris began to unload the largest, knobbliest, most segmented poo ever done at a dog show. Oh Gawd. While the crowd howled and redoubled their applause, Morris decided to really show how clever he was, by unsheathing his willy and wafting it around a bit. There's never a handy chasm to leap into when you need one, is there?

My morphine fog prevents exact recall, but I know that Morris's mega-poo seemed to run for  longer than most West-End shows and I distinctly remember that his willy uncannily resembled a stick of purple asparagus as it warmed to the applause of the crowd, before retreating inside the furry scabbard it calls home. Seconds of real time became hours of shame, as hordes of proper bull terrier owners looked on and guffawed at my grotesque pet. My clever speech now pointless, I took the microphone, mumbled something about, "...and people have the nerve to ask me if he's really as bad as I say." Then I left the show ring to hide in a corner that could never, ever, be dark enough.

After that little demo, things went swimmingly, and apart from Morris knocking over a trestle table  and burping in the faces of his fans - who'd paid 50p a go to give the hairy fool a cuddle, may I add - I was recovering nicely and actually beginning to enjoy the show. Then, Morris and I were called up to pick the winning raffle ticket. Even I don't believe what he did next.

The raffle ticketing bit went perfectly well, and we were off back to our little '50p A Cuddle' table, when Morris stopped at the edge of the show ring - and peed into a lady's handbag. Not a sprinkle, nor a tinkle, but a bloody great gush, like horses do. 'Spaloooshhh!' it went, straight into the lady's open bag, right on top of her food, car keys, purse and personals. My son was horrified and looked as though he was about to do a severe runner, until one of my parental laser-glances pinned him to his chair, because, you see, the lady whose bag it was - hadn't seen what Morris had done.

I'd seen every last drop of it. Kristopher had, too, as had a small gathering of Morris's fans, but the victim herself was blissfully unaware. Obviously, I immediately tapped the lady on the shoulder, with a gentlemanly, "Ahem! Terribly sorry m'dear, but it appears that my bull terrier has just pissed in your handbag.", and offered to make amends on the spot. Did I hell. I waited for the announcer to tell us that it was time to move outside, and scuttled off like the coward I am. The weather had warmed-up a treat, too, and I bet that lady's bag smelled lovely once the sun got at it. I only hope her sarnies were well wrapped, that's all.

So, if you were the lady with the handbag full of widdle, then I'm really, really, sorry. Tell you what, next year when we're at the show again, identify yourself and you can have a free snog. Me or Morris - take your pick. That'll be lovely for you, won't it?

Oh, I'm going again next year and so is Morris. Juliet Shaw says we'll be bigger than ever, with a proper stall selling Morrisabelia and everything, so you've got to come. This year he dumped in the show ring, waved his willy at the crowd and filled a lady's handbag with urine - who'd want to miss the encore to that?

Morris and Terry would like to thank all of the wonderful people who donated money to the Bull Terrier Club Welfare fund raiser and said so many nice things about Morris and his adventures. And sorry again to the lady with the handbag full of wee!

# Morris's Gift

## Morris makes a special new friend...

Aidan made my day, and Morris even behaved.

I've just had it confirmed by the fearsome controllers of editorial at Dogs Today, that it's not compulsory for me to have Morris's utter stupidity as the central theme to my every column. Cool. "I think I may include a selection of my poetry, this month.", I mused in reply to this revelation. "Don't take the bleedin' wossname - awright?", snarled the office girly in reply, probably manicuring her nails with the hatchet she undoubtedly keeps in her handbag.

Strong women (especially hatchet-carrying versions that growl) scare me to death, so you'll have to be deprived of my uplifting verse, in favour of a wee story that'll warm your cockles and seriously smile-up your rain-dreary faces.

Remember that report I did about last year's fund raising 'do' for Bull Terrier Welfare? Those of you now answering 'dunno what you're on about, mush', aren't helping me at all, you know. OK, I'll re-cap. Morris and I attended said fund-raiser and via the tremendous generosity of Morris's fans (oh yes, he's got fans, honest) we did very well. During the day, loads of folks came along to meet us and have photos done with Morris. Nobody wanted a pic with me, but I never mention it, actually, because I'm so classy and dignified and stuff.

Anyway, among Morris's well-wishers was a young lad called Aidan, who for some reason I referred to as 'Luke'. Aidan is blind and somehow Morris knew that this was one playmate who might not fully appreciate the usual full-on, bull terrier greeting. While Aidan got to know Morris through his fingertips, Morris stood quite still, his powerful frame becalmed by Aidan's gentle explorations. It was a remarkable and extremely emotional thing to watch and I was genuinely moved by what I saw.

I wrote of our encounter with Aidan, and, despite my clumsy mis-naming of him, Aidan recognised himself as his mum read aloud what I'd written. Aidan's mum then wrote to me, enclosing a letter from Aidan which was printed in Braille with mum's translation between the lines of raised dots. Again, I was moved by this charming young man. Aidan's letter has now been framed and hangs in my office as a reminder of the real reward of writing for a living.

I so wanted to give Aidan something in appreciation for his kindness, but I wanted it to be more than a photo, which could be described to him, or more words for someone else to read for him. Then, in an unprecedented blip of intelligence, I found the ideal solution.

Some months ago, an unfairly talented lady by the name of Alison Van Dyke had sent me a superb painted model of 'A Bully In A China Shop', depicting Morris in a spookily accurate pose, surrounded by smashed crockery. The piece is simply brilliant and is admired by doggy and non-doggy friends alike. Love it as I do, I nonetheless asked Alison if she'd be offended if I gave Bully In A China Shop to Aidan.

Alison had a mini-think and within seconds told me that she had a better idea. Well, it would be better than my idea, wouldn't it? I mean, look at the head from whence my ideas come - then consider the source of Alison's. S'obvious, innit?

Alison's idea was, indeed, a great one. She'd donate a limited edition of 'Bully On A Surfboard', which, apart from being a right larf, is an even more 'tactile' representation of a bull terrier. This lady has perfectly captured the concentrated essence of bull terrier, in her point-perfect model, virtually bringing the statue to life in the process. What a fine bit of work it is. Alison then told me she planned to personalise her gift to Aidan by writing his name in Braille on the base. Beyond being hugely talented as an artist, Alison Van Dyke is even more stupendously blessed as a human being. Blush away, Alison, you deserve it, girl. A round of applause for this lovely lady, please. Ithenkyew!

I bound the surfing bully in most of the western hemisphere's bubblewrap output and parcel-forced it to Aidan's house in time for Christmas morning. We magazine contributors have to work months ahead of schedule, so I can't relay

Aidan's reaction to his Bully On A Surfboard, but his mum's seen it and she assures me that her son will be overjoyed. I bet he will, too.

Now, wasn't that a nice story, ladies and gentlemen? See, my Morris isn't all mayhem and moronic meanderings. Mostly, but not all. OK, so yesterday he ate another plug - pins, fuse, plastic casing, the lot. At least it wasn't a plugged-in plug, though, and he didn't even burn the house down or anything. Morris could well be reaching that point in his life where maturity overcomes reckless behavior, you know. Whaddaya mean, 'and you could be the next teen-pop sensation, you fat old git.' You really mustn't be so sceptical, you know. Besides, I'd make a right-good Westlife'er, I would. "Hiiiiiiyyyym flyyyyy-eeeeng widdout weeeeeengs!" See?

# Snail Seizer

## Morris comes out of his shell...

As I write, Morris is recovering. He's been through trauma, bless'im, and I daresay he requires several months of designer counseling. He'll not be getting a minute of it, though, because he is a git of the purest order and this particular trauma was entirely his fault. Now there's a shock. Not.

Briefly, Morris got himself entangled in a roll of wire mesh, cutting his mouth, ear and several of the squishy areas between his toes. The mesh was innocent of any attack, unlike Morris, who'd taken a raging dislike to the fact that it was preventing him from snacking on snails. You'll require a re-run of that last bit, then.

Morris discovered that huge quantities of garden snails live within the fronds of a pair of grassy clumps which stand, sentry-like on each side of our shed's porch. Well, it isn't a porch, it's the space behind the ivy-occupied trellis where all of the things we'll never use again are carefully stored until we don't need them. Anyway, after a week of traditional summer rain, Morris noticed that our back garden was a-glisten with the shiny shells and trails of various gastropods - posh name for slugs and snails - literally means 'stomach-foot' - fascinating, isn't it? Please yourselves.

No bloodhound, he, but even Morris can track a snail as it bolts for cover. It appears that the majority of our gastros' hot-pod it for the shelter of those grassy outcrops whenever hungry thrushes or some other danger threatens. As you will know, your cuddly thrush spends its waking hours beating the hell out of snails via a technique which can only be described as 'smashing them against a handy rock'. Is it any wonder that snails go warp-four for cover as soon as anything spooks them?

Morris's skill, speed and determination kept him locked onto one such fleeing snail, which eventually led him to the mother of all mollusc conventions amid the friendly fronds of our grassy stuff.. Each bucket-sized clump somehow holds around two gallons of snails and these plants are such des-res's, that, having elbowed their way to the prestigious basement area, new tenants will cement themselves together in knobbly lumps of snailkind rather than seek pastures new. About the size of a golf ball, these conglomerations represent the snail equivalent of a thrush-proof apartment block, and I imagine poorer snails look upon them with multi-eyed envy.

Now, concentrate on those crunchy, juicy, sticky bundles of gastropod fun for a moment, please. Can you picture Morris mouthing them like a sort of industrial-strength Ferrero Roche? You can, can't you? Oh yes.

We first discovered Morris's obsession with munching snail-bundles when pieces of shell began to appear in his poo. Studying Morris's poo is a constant in our lives. It's the means by which we trace his acts of destruction, and pre-empt his requirement for veterinary treatment. Thus, intertwined ivy fronds will usually mean we're on stand-by for a trip to the vet's, while electrical cable clippings must trigger a full-scale seek-and-isolate maneuver. After long experience and repeated false alarms, polystyrene packaging, Herself's tights, pebbles, items of jewelry and pages of assorted literature are now judged on their merits and usually considered passive, having emerged safely. So, when silvery splinters of snail shrapnel winked at us from one of Morris's mounds, it was a matter for concern and debate.

Before a skillful poke with a stick revealed the silver splinters as sections of snail house, Herself immediately accused Morris of eating light bulbs. I thought he'd found the Christmas tree decorations I'd stashed in the shed, and my mother immediately leapt to Morris's defense by declaring that 'his diet must lack calcium or vitamin C or something.' She trots out this catch-all excuse for every crime my dog commits. Morris eats the gearknob of Herself's car - he's lacking roughage. Morris snaffles a carton of cream from the doorstep - he's lactose-deficient. Herself reckons that my mum's diagnosis will only be correct if Morris ever trots to the butchers' and scoffs a hundredweight of brains. That's cruel, isn't it everyone?

Having identified Morris as a major consumer of snails, it was my job to curtail his new habit before it either killed him or ruined a carpet. Every new problem Morris causes seems to end in ruined carpet and we've just had another new one installed. My fix therefore had to be quick.

A pair of swift wraparounds with large-mesh wire netting, secured by sturdy stakes, annexed the grassy clumps, keeping out Morris's stupid face, while allowing the snails their sanctuary. 'Eventually', I told Herself, 'the leaves will grow through the mesh and it'll become invisible, but it'll still keep Morris from eating the snails.'
'How very Titchmarsh', she said, pretending not to be impressed by my genius.

Morris wasn't impressed by it at all. Finding himself cut off from his essential snail supply he did what all brainless life forms do when thought and strategy are required - he launched a full-frontal attack. My sturdy stakes were plucked from the ground like lollipop sticks and Morris set about turning galvanised mesh into lots of single strands of assaulted wire. Owners of bull terriers will attest to the phenomenal strength and determination of their pets, and when this is aligned to a pain threshold that is off the scale plus no sense whatsoever, the result absolutely must be damage of the highest order.

Morris prefers to damage most things in silence, so I was only alerted to the situation by the sound of a snail, hurled from rest by Morris shaking the mesh like a rat, impacting on my office window. By then, Morris was bleeding heavily from wounds to his mouth and paws, as the mesh became stressed and blessed with the slicing ability of cheesewire under the force of the attack.

Cue another visit to the vet, while my sons evicted snails, wire and grass clumps from our garden. I have only just returned from the vet, who did his usual patch-up job on Morris, while mugging me for the compulsory, eye-watering fee. All caused by a few snails. I ask you. Never mind about Morris being traumatised, what about me? I think I need some brandy. A couple of slugs should do the trick. Geddit? As I said - please yourselves.

# The Expert

## Sit back and learn, folks…

I met a local expert on bull terriers the other evening. In fact he wasn't just 'an' expert – he was 'the' expert. He knew everything about them. More, in fact, 'than any of them Mickey Mouse experts wot's in them dog books an' that'. Like most self-appointed gurus, he wasn't in the least reluctant to share his vast store of knowledge, and I obviously consider myself fortunate to have drifted into his orbit.

During my audience with this monument to lower primate inter-breeding, I learned much. I believe it's only fair that I spread the gospel of St. Neanderthal among the readership of this 'dog book', in the hope that its Mickey Mouse contingent might learn a few things. You may all consider yourselves extremely fortunate, for while you may snigger at St. Nean's preachings from the comfort of your sitting-room upholstery, I received his wisdom via exhalations of beer-breath and Old Blacklung tobacco. Trust me, that's the last time I walk Morris to that pub. Settle back now, for you are about to be informed.

### Locking Jaws
'See them dogs? They got jaws wot lock togevva. S'right. See, when they bites sunnink, there's a special bone wot clicks down an' locks their jaws shut. That's why you can't never get 'em orf once they've took 'old, see? Only way they gets to let go is to bite a bit 'arder an' that lets the little bone click out so their jaws can open. Din'tchu know that?'
I said that I didn't. He was sympathetic toward my ignorance and qualified it with, 'Yeah, well I spec' you reads them dog books an' that, don'tcha? Well, them lot won't tell you what bull terriers are all about, mate. I'll tell you summin' else an'all….'

### Bullies Can't Swim
'See them dogs? They can 'ardly swim. You know why? It's coz their bones are so 'eavy that they got a job to not-sink. Straight up. I bet your dog 'ates going in the water, dunnee?'

I told the gentleman that Morris would swim to France given the opportunity, but the perfect explanation for this was but another combination belch of Heineken and rancid smoke away.

'THAT'S coz your dog ain't a proper bull terrier, though, innit? I mean, no offense like, but 'ee's one of them pedigree dogs ennee? Not a proper 'un. Proper 'uns is so 'eavy that they're nearly all bone an' muscle, whereas you dog's fat, ain't 'ee?'

Morris is hardly in perfect sporting trim, but he's a long way from fat and has a couple of Arnie's worth of muscle on him. Oh well, my dog obviously falls below the quality expected by the all-knowing St. Nean'. I'll just have to live with it. Meanwhile, he had more revelations.

### Special Eyes
'See them dogs? They got eyes like no uvver dog, they 'ave. Them dogs 'as eyes that go right back in their 'eads. For when they're fightin', see? Yeah, wot 'appens is that when them dogs is 'avin' a scrap, they pulls their eyes into special sockets an' a fing comes down over 'em to protect 'em.'

I told him that he may be confusing bull terriers with sharks, which is an easy mistake to make given the similarities in mental capacity and table manners. He assured me that 'his mate knew a vet, wot told 'im about the eyes fing. Pukkah, mate, they got well-funny eyes. Take it from me.' At this point, the only thing I wished to take from him was his next 20 minutes of breathing. But, pursuing his quest for my enlightenment, he had further pearls to cast.

### The Dangers Of Exercise
'See them dogs? Well, if you let's 'em run abaht too much they gets muscle-bound and can't 'ardly walk. S'true. They've been bred wiv too much muscle on 'em, see? So, if you don't keep an eye on 'em, it all builds up too much an' they goes bandy-legged an' can't run. Yours is alright, like, coz 'ees fat an' that. But you deffenly needs to be careful wiv proper 'uns.'

By now he was theatrically draining his long-empty glass every 30 seconds or so, in a pantomime hint that he'd like me to buy him a drink. After dispensing such wisdom to me it was surely right that I should return the gesture with lager. As it was, he had more chance of me giving him a love-bite. As a final punt for a pint, the ultimate bull terrier expert leaned forward, and, direct from his personal beer-smoke fug, I was privy to one of the best-kept secrets of the canine world. I bet the Mickey Mouse contingent of this dog-book will count themselves equally blessed.

### Turbo Spots
'See them dogs? Them spots on their belly? Well, they're not spots like wot ordinary dogs've got. Nah, them spots is made of special fat wot burns fast and gives them dogs a quick boost of energy when they needs it, like when they're fightin' an' that. Oh yeah, that's the real secret of why them dogs never runs out of energy. Unless they uses up all their fat-spots a'course.'

There you go. I trust you're all impressed, especially the bull terrier owners among you. I know I was. My only regret was that Morris couldn't fully absorb what his ultimate expert was saying. How comforting it would surely have been for my dog to have finally found a life form that's even more daft than himself.

# Drip Ahoy!

## Nothing ever goes swimmingly with Morris…

If he goes in – it's full steam ahead until he hits the other side..

When you take your normal pet for a dip at a dog-friendly seaside, you bring an extra towel. When I take Morris, I need an offshore powerboat, a lasso and a Thick Mutt Importation Licence, in case the boat and rope let me down. You see, although Morris is without doubt, the strongest, most determined swimmer in canine history, the sad fact is - he can only do it in one direction.

Morris can't manouvre - fact. The dopey dog's not for turning. He can't come about, tack to starboard, or do anything navigational on the windward side, port bow or leeward wossname. Once into his stroke, Morris ploughs an arrow-straight, water-furrow until his keel hits something solid. On a lake or river, that will usually turn out to be the opposite bank. In the sea, I could well be looking at Madagascar.

# A Guide Dog For The Thick

This is not a restful situation for me. You see, as with everything Morris, there's no easy solution to his unilateral bathing policy and a day at the seaside is a most fraughtsome trial. Oh I know what you're thinking. 'If, when the Does are disporting themselves on Brighton beach and Morris happens to strike out for Europe in general, why doesn't that useless writer-bloke simply pop into the surf and point poor Morris back toward Blighty.' That's it, isn't it? Well, it's not 'it' or anything like 'it', as a matter of fact. It isn't even 'it'ish', if you really want to know.

You see, once his doggy-paddle rhythm is established, Morris can outpace the average marlin. Flipper himself would be knackered trying to keep up with the water-borne version of my dog and a team of wild seahorses couldn't turn him back to his point of origin. Trust me, folks, Morris is the one who put the 'bark;' in embarkation. The only chance I have, lies with early interception. If I can get Morris in a headlock before those paddle-wheel feet accelerate to full-ahead, I can reclaim him without H. M. Customs getting involved. Should my attention wander for the time it takes Morris's engine room to power-up his pistoning pads - it's time to call the Coastguard.

Perhaps the less Morris-acquainted among you may harbour ('harbour' - geddit? keep the maritime motif going, Tel-boy) the notion that he'd eventually become fed-up with being a salty seadog and return to the ones that love him so dear? Nope, won't happen. I've already tested this one, and it was pretty scary. There was nothing pretty about it, actually, it was just scary. Morris went for a dip in a three-acre lake, surged to the opposite bank like a pink-testicled torpedo, then, with his chest against a gravel outcrop and his feet treading water, he swam on the spot for three-quarters of an hour. I sat on the bank, timing him, my dismay and wonder gathering compound interest by the minute.

Morris didn't stop swimming. I stopped him. Left to his own devices, he'd have spent the night paddling his stationary paddle, while his permanently stationary brain told him to carry on until winter set in and the lake froze. I presume he would have then hibernated until the spring thaw, whereupon the new risen sun would have re-energised him and he'd take up where he left off. This prediction is far more realistic than the possibility of Morris angling his fat bum a tad to one side and swimming toward a shallow spot. He wouldn't even deviate from his 180-degree course when I dislodged him with the elongated walking stick I carry whenever I walk him close to water.

Every time I prodded him off the promontory with my rubber-tipped boat hook, he re-docked at precisely the same position, chin on dry land, legs robotically churning, tail rudder set for straight ahead. Eventually, I could stand it no longer and I hooked the handle of my stick through his collar and hoiked him out. He simply did one of those shudder-shakes that hopeless dogs think (wrongly) will rid them of excess water, and bounded off as though he'd just paddled through a deep'ish puddle. Silently, my arms spread wide, I looked toward heaven, a venue at which I've enquired so many times before, begging the Almighty to at least give me a clue. Sadly, He was out and, like my dog, I remain clueless.

So, not only do I have the normal worries associated with owning a dog, and a dog which happens to be a bull terrier, and a bull terrier which happens to have done a brain-swap with a fruit fly called Dopey, I also have the stress of knowing that my particular dog is a shipping hazard. While the rest of you can sort out a cosy insurance scheme with 'Doggyrisk' or 'Puppy Plan', I've got to sit around a table with a gang of suits from Lloyds Of London in case Morris collides with a supertanker. He's a buoy, that Morris, eh?

# Today The Co-Op, Tomorrow The World!

## Fame at last...

Morris and I are famous - it's official. We have been recognised in the Co-op car park. Being proper stars, we graciously gave our time and attention to our adoring fan. Admittedly, that's 'fan' singular, but she obviously represents the trickle that will become the flood.

There we were, loitering by the trolley-corral, giggling to ourselves like the spottiest of schoolboys every time someone rammed a trolley up the bottom of the one tethered ahead of it. By the way, this trolley-mating ritual is doubly hilarious when the cart-wrangler doesn't ram hard enough and has to have a few runs at it. Watch next time you're at the supermarket. Anyway, we were having a right good snigger at the bonking trolleys when an incredibly kind and unfairly attractive young lady - who will undoubtedly be reading this, oh yes - began to stare at us.

I thought perhaps my giggling and Morris' break-dancing (that lie-on-your-back-and-squiggle-like-a-fish move Bull Terriers do when having a good time) had alarmed the poor girl, but not a bit of it. We had been spotted fair and square, and she flourished her copy of Dogs Today to prove it.

It was the one in which Morris had been asked to demolish a selection of chewy toys, where the main cover line screamed 'BALLS' in letters a subtle two inches high. I'd been press-ganged by the DT editor (who had better watch out if a Dangerous Editors' Act ever comes about) into appearing alongside Morris in a microscopic photo accompanying that month's main feature. This expanded on the coverline a smidgen, to the tune of 'OH, BALLS!', again writ large, only this time in red, with a fine upstanding exclamation mark.

Was this embarrassing or what? I was only wearing the same shirt and jeans I had on in the photo. Our fan didn't seem too bothered, though. She was more amused by the fact that she'd been reading the magazine in the car when us two mega-stars just appeared in public, without bodyguard, limo or paparazzi. A-blimmin'-mazing and no mistake.

Morris was fussed over and I was occasionally spoken to for the next 10 minutes, during which it emerged our fan 'absolutely loved' Bull Terriers, thought Morris was 'absolutely wonderful' and 'absolutely absolutely' couldn't understand how anyone could think a handsome dog like Morris was ugly. Not a mention of my fine self, or the articles I tear from my tortured soul every month, just to make Morris a star.

Never one merely to fish for compliments, I began to deploy the trawl net. "Nice to see the old articles are appreciated after all the hard work that goes into them - ha ha.", I lobbed in the 'ha ha' to make it sound as though I was only joking, really, in case such a pathetic plea for acknowledgement brought the scorn it deserved. This time my trawl net came up empty, and our fan merely smiled the smile the Queen wears when 'entertained' by gyrating hordes of native dancers during state visits.

I was almost relieved when Herself (my wife, not the Queen) came trundling toward us, trolley laden with Co-Operation, and keen to get it all packed into the car. Our fan told Herself how she'd just been admiring Morris and how she found him "even more handsome in real life than he is in his photo". The hairy git (Morris, not Herself) obviously lapped this up, while I was told to decant the shopping and take the trolley to be mated.

By the time I came back, our fan had gone and Herself had the engine running. "What's it like being hero-worshipped then?" she asked as she grounded the new exhaust-pipe on the first 15 Co-Op speed humps. "Why don't you ask the slavering idiot in the back?" I replied in that dignified way of mine.

Do you know, despite a bit of a bad start, I think I'm really cut out for this being-famous lark. I've already developed an attitude. I can throw tantrums like a told-off teenager - and who on this earth has more dope-related problems than Morris causes me?

# Things Are What They Used To Be

## Morris and his fleeting fixations...

Morris has 'things' about things. All sorts of things, actually. His latest thing is about pasta and he'll move heaven, earth and kitchen appliances to get his thing-fix. Less than an hour ago his pasta-detecting radar sussed a packet of après-sell-by macaroni in the bin. Morris mugged the bin, inhaled the macaroni in seconds (plus a box of prehistoric mince pies) and he's just slurped down a gallon of water. As I write, Morris is a canine zeppelin. His abdomen is inflating to critical pressure, after which he'll deflate, via either the world's most spectacular display of projectile vomiting, or the mega-poo session from hell.

I'll be here, a'watching and awaiting the deflation as I always do, worried sick while Morris sleeps in blissful ignorance of what he's done to himself. He's sprawled on his bed, snoring like an elephant seal, and auto-farting to stabilize his internal pressure. I'm writing this, enveloped in what's emerging from Morris's safety valve, and confirming to myself yet again that I am truly the saddest person I know.

Morris's past 'things' have included the mouse that he thought lived in the shed, my underpants, boating shoes, a very electric cattle fence, a purple-plumed feather duster, the wedges that held my computer table together and several tons of highland cattle, complete with disembowelment-standard horns and permanent bovine PMT.

Most of these things he has things about are eventually chewed up and eaten. Obviously, he didn't eat the highland cattle (that would be silly) so he made the best of it by eating the dung they produced. As for the electric fence, well, he did chew that up but I got to him before he could swallow anything significant. I don't know if Morris ate the mouse in the shed or not, but the rest of those things I mentioned, plus many, many, more, certainly went the shark's gob  route to oblivion.

In the early days when I still had a functioning brain, I'd do all manner of earnest research into Morris's obsessions but I rarely bother these days. The fact is, every now and then he locks his mental tractor beam onto something and it occupies his every non-thought. When a head's as empty as the one Morris uses, it doesn't take much to occupy it.

There's absolutely no point in trying to predict where the next 'thing' will come from, either. While Morris was obsessing about my underpants – only the worn, previously moist ones, thanks – I maintained such a focus on my discarded Y-fronts and the laundry basket which acted as their storage silo, that I completely failed to intercept an incoming 'thing' and Morris was in love with the shed-mouse before I knew it. Even as I endured a round-the-clock pants-watch on the laundry basket, Morris was bulldozing our freezer into a disconnected meltdown, to get at the mouse that lived behind it.

He once had a brief and painful 'thing' with a local cat, and from this particular obsession I learned a great deal – all of it extremely disappointing. Morris would see, hear or smell (the smart money was on the latter) the cat approaching, and he'd poke his big nose through the slats in our side gate, the better to sniff his latest 'thing'. The cat would approach Morris, set itself for maximum leverage, and, savouring every swipe, proceed to reduce Morris's nose to tatters

# Doing...'Thingy'

## Parental discretion advised...

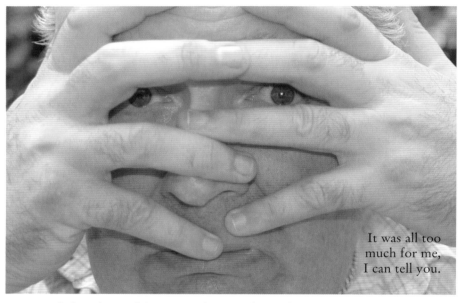

It was all too much for me, I can tell you.

My Morris has done 'thingy' you know. That's thingy singular. Like, just the once thanks very much - but it was with a girly, so he's earned the right to tell 'goorn my san' stories to the lads over a boozy curry of a Friday night. And unlike most, Morris won't be making it up, because I was there when it happened.

I saw him pull the bird in question. I saw him push her quite a bit as well, and I gawped in horror as he trundled her around like a wheelbarrow. I even saw him become half of a Pushme-pullyou. You frequent witnesses to dog-thingy will know what I'm talking about and doubtless you'll be astonished at my prudish references to what we've been asked to believe is a perfectly natural act.

Well it didn't look very natural when Morris did it.

I'll set the pre-thingy scene for you, then the sheer toe-curlingness of it all will be laid bare, so to speak. Believe it or not, our Morris is a bit of a looker. Thick he may be, but he's one seriously happenin' hunk and several bull terrier owners have approached me with thingy on their minds. One such overture came from a lady who owns a house so large, that you have to change the time on your watch if you intend to walk the entire hall carpet. This distinguished lady wanted Morris to thingy her Lucy within the week and there was no time to lose.

I consulted Herself on the matter and she adopted her usual positive stance where matters of Morris are concerned.

'If anyone is mad enough to want to replicate that bloody dog - they must be even stupider than he is.' Thank you my Dear. Remind me to top-up your carafe of evening primrose oil before I go.

Thus it was that one snowy winter's eve, the virginal Morris found himself at the desperately posh home of Mrs. Gertrude Calloway, whose dear departed had been huge in music or somesuch. Anyway, 'call me Trudi' now devoted herself to her dogs, cats and causes. The cause before her this evening, was to get Morris and Lucy productively rogering.

Now, call me old Mr. Silly, but I expected to lob Morris and Lucy into one of Trudi's empty stables and leave them to it. I imagined that Trudi and I would share a sherry or two, gossip a bit, then retrieve the happy couple after their half an hour's worth of happy coupling. 'Aaay naaay Terry. The whole thing has to be soopahvised, especially with bullies. Have you never seen it done?'

Well of course I'd seen it done hadn't I? It's just that where I grew up, every time it was done, someone would come out and throw a bucket of water over those that were doing it. I'd seen it done plenty of times. It's just that I'd never seen it encouraged that's all.

What followed was the most embarrassing episode of my entire life - bar none.

Trudi was pleased that when introduced in the games room, Morris and Lucy actually wanted to get it together in the rumpy-pumpy department, rather than bite lumps out of each other. Morris was more than pleased, because with my own eyes I actually saw the creature from Alien begin to emerge from his bits. It was like that advert for the TV Times - 'I never knew there was so much in it.' Where the hell he'd stored that lot I'll never know, but there it was, and apart from a few er...'directional' problems, he seemed to know what it was all for as well.

I just wanted to apologise for it. I mean, in front of a posh woman and all, when Trudi did something that nearly made me faint. Get this. While Morris was mid piggy-back with Lucy and frantically stabbing thin air with the Alien, Trudi knelt down and using her professionally manicured hand...aimed it for him! And to think she could have offered me a sandwich.

'Oh good', said Trudi, as most of the Alien docked with Lucy. 'Oh God', said I, as another gallon of sweat fell away and sizzled on the games room floor. I'd had enough by now and slipped gratefully into the courtyard where a cooling carpet of snow had fallen. I literally steamed with embarrassment, yet couldn't resist a peek through the window at the goings-on. Morris and Lucy, still nailed together by the Alien, now stood tail-to-tail, panting, while Trudi stroked their heads reassuringly.

Ten interminable minutes later, Morris was led out to join me and as Trudi enthused over this 'text-book' mating, I watched awe-struck as Morris's Alien burned a trail through the snow before climbing back into its furry hangar. For the first and last time if I've got anything to do with it.

Finally it was over and I could breathe the shame-free air of liberty. And you can bet I waved good-bye to 'call me Trudi', rather than shake her guiding hand.

# Cross Wires

## I'm being positively negative toward Morris...

I'm ignoring Morris again at the moment, and he hates it more than any other ineffective punishment I've ever inflicted upon him. I believe that I've finally perfected the art of disregarding Morris, to a point where I may award myself a masters degree in ignor-ance. Yes, that sounds about right. Maybe one day I'll take my place among the dons of disregard, and become a full-blown Ignoramus Academicus. Most likely, I think you'll agree.

This latest bout of 'You don't exist- you git', was visited upon Morris due to his deliberate snip-biting of the telephone cables which connect my office to the real world, where lives (for the most part) my editors, publishers and remote galaxy of friends, family and e-chums. Two cables were sheared when Morris retaliated to the unfair washing of his bedding and the resulting destruction of the essential smells with which he strives to anoint it.

Oh yes, it was a deliberate act of payback, all right. Within seconds of the freshly laundered sleeping gear being arranged in his bed, Morris swaggered over to it, sniffed it, then pretended to find the cleansing residue of Ariel Ultra so revolting, that he started gagging and sneezing all over the place. "You...are...a...tart.", I counseled, zapping Morris with my most disdainful sneer. He considered his options for a second - which is his absolute consideration-duration - slunk to the corner of my office, and snipped the telephone cables as casually as a normal dog would snaffle an unguarded tidbit.

Bull terriers can do this with uncanny precision. The cables barely twitched, no wall plugs were disturbed or telephones dislodged, yet those scarcely opened jaws had sheared both flexes like a pair of Do-It-All's sharpest secateurs. I didn't even know he'd done it, until my next outgoing e-mail refused to set foot outside the door. Obviously, I am a total techno-wizard where computers are concerned, and immediately launched my comprehensive threats, pleas and wailing routine. The next phase of this impressive demo' of my I.T. expertise is a head-butt to the monitor, and I was in the middle of a final warning before delivering it, when Morris tried to escape.

When they actually know that they've done something wrong - for most times they don't - bull terriers adopt the most over-done expressions of pantomime guilt since Bill Clinton went on telly and remembered that he'd campaigned a tad too vigorously in Monica's constituency. Morris practically does a belly crawl, elevated to pure melodrama by horizontal ears, and a facial expression which can only be described as an oily cringe. In guilt mode, Morris looks like an even more hangdog Dot Cotton. One glance at his sorry retreat confirmed that he'd done something, and retracing his movements led me to the sliced wires. Sussed!

Thus Morris and I find ourselves at the present impasse of ignoring each other. Oh, he'd make friends in a slobbering second but I'm not ready to re-commit to him, yet. I know that's how I feel because I saw someone just like me on Opra the other day. Or was it Jenny Jones? Charlie Dimmock wasn't in it, I'm sure of that. Neither was Jonathon Ross, so it was definitely a U.S. show, then. Anyway, I learned that Morris and I have 'issues' and we need to seek 'closure', which was nice to know. Then I thought, if only Morris hadn't used his shark's gob to perform 'closure' on my telephone wires, we'd have no bloody 'issue' at all.

I can even ignore Morris when I take him for a walk, you know. He knows I'm upset,  because he won't look at me, but he keeps swiveling his piggy eyeballs sideways to sneak a peek to see if I'm still narked. He hates being scowled at, too, so, in the cultured terminology of my children, I 'give him evils' to let him know that the status is still very much quo. And if you think I'm making too much of what is surely Morris's quintillionth misdemeanor, kindly think very again.

As Morris's pack leader, every physical syllable of my body language is hugely significant to him. He'd know I was not a happy bunny, even if I tried to pretend otherwise. That momentary slump of my shoulders, the micro-bowing of my head, and the subtle dragging of my disaster-weary feet as I leave the scene of his latest crime, all speak volumes to Morris, making my involuntary groaning of 'Awwww gaaaaawwwwwd!' hardly worthwhile, really.

Morris's reading of me is so finely tuned, that he senses I'm ready to stop ignoring him, even before I've made my decision. As I type this very line, he's lying on his back and fish-wiggling toward me, grinning his upside-down grin and scoping me out for the first sign of a forgiving gesture. He's so sure I'm about to crack. What do you think? Shall I forgive him, yet again? Shall I? I suppose I should, really. Shouldn't I?

WELL I'M NOT GOING TO!!! Ha, ha. He didn't read that one. I win!

# Tong-Tied

## Morris finds that tongs are a tough act to swallow...

**Dateline: 3pm a few Wednesdays ago.**
Dedicated publishing executive, Terry Doe is giving his all at the office by attempting a quintuple spin in his new chair. He'd already managed a magnificent four rotations but was beginning to feel sick and was winding up for one last mega-twist - when the phone bleeped and ruined his concentration. It was Herself. "Come home right now, Morris is choking to death. He's eaten something ridiculous and I can't get hold of the vet."

You simply will not believe how many times I've had to pull dangerous things out of here.

Terry takes up the story:

"Can't you get hold of whatever's choking him, and hoik it out?" I said, already in control of the situation. "I can't get within five bloody yards of him! Unless you can tell me where to find a tranquiliser gun, you'd better get here soon, or he's going to die. I am not joking." When she's not joking, it means she's serious and it's my fault. So I abandoned my brave office chair rotation record attempt and left the office in a single bound, pointing the family Citroen toward home at a most illegal rate.

I hit our driveway running, entering the house to find Morris staggering around in drunken distress and 'karking' like a sea lion. Morris can kark louder than most dogs bark and has always enjoyed a good puke, but this time he was in serious trouble. I first suspected poison, but his efforts to kark-out whatever was depriving him of breath, told me otherwise. I grabbed him by the bottom jaw, wrenched open his mouth like a lion tamer of old and saw to my horror a huge piece of metal sticking out of his throat.

Plunging in my hand, I tried to grasp the metal between my fingertips, which only succeeded in making Morris swallow hard and force the lump of shiny steel even deeper into his throat. Morris had passed out by now and his breath was coming in shudders, so with little or no breath going in, it could only be a matter of minutes before even his brain became starved of oxygen. I had to do something successful - and now.

I gave up my fingertip exploration of Morris's esophagus and scaling the stairs in three bounds, I ransacked my boys' fishing kit for the sturdy pair of artery forceps they use to unhook pike. On my way back to Morris, I grabbed a bottle of shampoo as I flew past the bathroom cabinet and prepared for a literal do-or-die sitting-room floor operation.

Cranking open his jaws, I wedged in the shampoo bottle to keep the access open, while probing around the saliva covered pinkness of Morris's throat with the half-open forceps. Morris was barely twitching by this time and I thought we'd lost him for sure, when a metallic 'clunk' from the forceps gave us one last chance to save the day. My fingers were numb as I struggled to lock the forceps over the now invisible metalwork, but somehow I clamped them down and watched in frantic relief as the toothed ratchet on the handles engaged with a positive 'clack'.

I pulled with steady pressure, while even in his unconscious state, Morris made life as difficult as possible for me by doing reflex-swallows every two seconds. Finally, there was movement from the forceps, followed seconds later by a hideous 'ploop' as Morris's constricted throat gave up its grip on the steel intrusion and showered me with bile.

Safely clamped within the sturdy chrome jaws of the forceps was a flat piece of spring steel, which had once been the driving force behind my bar-b-que tongs. Morris had mangled and discarded the rest of the tongs, before swallowing the spring and blocking off his windpipe a treat.

Morris began to inflate within seconds of the spring's removal, while I, slimed in bile and slobber, watched in open-mouthed anxiety for signs that the blessed spark of life might somehow be rekindled. Then, he leapt to his feet, shook himself as though waking from a fireside nap and went over to drink from his water bowl. "Wha...but....how...uuuh..." and similar bright queries stuttered from my still-open mouth, as I silently scraped the green, frothy mess from my shirt front. Morris trotted past a couple of times, bright as a button, looking at me as though I was a bit strange and resenting my scowls as I cleaned up the mess he'd made me make.

Suddenly, from the kitchen came the sound of a bull terrier choking to death. Oh, no. I'd ruptured a blood vessel in his throat, I knew I had. His lungs were filling up with arterial blood and he would die in my arms, the victim of my brutish mishandling of a pair of forceps. Er...no, not quite. You see, Morris had found a monstrous ball of silver foil in the bin, and he was busily trying to ram it down the very throat that I'd so recently saved his useless life by unblocking.

This time, screaming "BLAAAAAADEEEE HELLLL DOG!!!", was my life-saving method of choice. Next time, I think I'll just lob Morris the forceps and sod-off down the pub. Either that, or his suicide attempts will be the death of me.

# Meeting One's Public

## We've gone all showbiz...

Luvvies, daaaahlings, best-best friends and possibly a few of you ordinary little people, too, I shouldn't wonder. Kissyhugs and both-cheek, mwah-mwahs to you all. Obviously I love each and every one of you guys and there's not a member of my readership who isn't my dearest chum. If I can ever inspire you further, you have only to ask. Then praise me lavishly. Oh, and let's only talk about me, OK?

Morris and I have been doing the micro-celeb bit at the Bull Terrier Club Fundraiser day again. You'd never guess, would you? I mean, despite the glory, adulation and the constant attention of our adoring masses - all of it thoroughly deserved, natch - Mo' and me are simply not affected by it at all. 'Mazing, yah? As I said to my good mate (Editor: bung in a famous name, here - they'll never know) only the other day, "Sweetie", I said (Oi, Ed - best make sure it's a girly, there's a love) "Isn't it tooooo soooooper that we've remained the approachable genius's we started out as?" My famous friend agreed, God bless her, commenting that she really didn't know how I keep my dainty size 12's planted so firmly on the ground. "Me neither, Precious-Dearie", I remarked, just like we working class, salt of the earth folk do. It was such a typical moment for me, lately. Now that Morris and I are famous, like.

(Ouch!!!)

Bleed'nell! Herself's just infiltrated my office in that creeping-Nazi way of hers, and repeatedly batted me about the head with a soft furnishing. She'd been reading this over my shoulder (shows her lack of breeding) and she's just called me a pretentious git. I'm crushed. So are at least three of my neck vertebrae and approximately two of my cheekbones. Morris got away scot-free, as usual, on account of Herself not being able to get to him once he makes it behind my filing cabinet. I really must try that one day.

As a consequence of this assault, and to avoid permanent structural damage, I have been forced to drop my preferred persona of Terence Upshot-Bagley-Doe-Smythe-Wossname, proper famous writer-bloke of this parish, in favour of plain old Terry Doe, alleged owner of Morris, numb-nuts to the masses. Such is fame, oh curse its fleeting embrace.

So, what went on at this year's Bully bash, then? Tons, that's what, and all of it absolutely ber-illiant with a capital 'BER'. Upon arrival at the natural wonder that is White Waltham in high summer, Morris and I alighted from the car and strode imposingly... (ouch!, OK, Goebbels, you win!)...over to the orchard where the stalls were sited, we were met by a huge banner inviting the show-goers to come and meet us. Spooky or what? I'd brought Stephen, my youngest, with me and his reaction to the sight of that banner summed-up the respect my family hold for my position within the writing establishment.

"Wot - people want to meet you?" he sneered, reverently. "Bet it's Morris they really want to meet - betcha any money." I allowed the boy his delusion, after all, my throng of awaiting fans would soon make a mockery of the poor child's cynical prediction. Well they would, had he been even slightly wrong. Tragically, the little sod had it dead right and Morris was engulfed by well-wishers whilst I stood around and smiled the smile of the bloke with no partner during the last waltz. Oh it's no good feeling sorry for me now. Too late by a long chalk, that is.

More shocks were to follow as I watched bales of what Juliet Shaw, fearsome organisor of my attendance at the show, calls 'Morris-a-belia' being purchased by those who enjoy his stories. I kid you not, there were Morris T-shirts (I bought Herself one - ha, ha!), Morris key-rings, Morris greetings cards and even Morris soap and flannel sets. Juliet had sorted it all, and the sales raised a nice few quid for bull terrier welfare. Well-done that lady, and thanks so much to all of you that bought or ordered stuff.

Meanwhile, I was busily engaged taking photos for dozens of people who requested a piccy with Morris. How many wanted a piccy with me? Exactly none. And still none after a re-count. Not a one of you. If Herself wasn't standing behind me right now, armed to the teeth with that tasseled death-cushion of hers, I'd tell you all what perfect beasts you are. Fancy slobbering all over Morris, while I was press-ganged into using your cameras to record it all for you. (May I risk a 'Don't you realise who I am?' at this point, Dear? Thought not.)

There was so much wonderfulness going down at that event - who could ever forget the bully fancy dress? - that the afternoon was gone before I knew it. Apart from continually pee-ing up my leg (hooray - a brand new trait, unveiled especially for the show) Morris was nothing short of magnificent. Even when he was...ahem...shall we say 'treated roughly' by a miniature bully who shall remain nameless, Morris didn't put a foot, or a bum, or even a willy wrong this year. His gentle reaction during his meetings with young Aidan, Morris's new special friend, had me near to tears with appreciation for his wonderful temperament. I'm sure Aidan enjoyed these meetings, too, and I'd very much like to hear from him if he's reading this.

All around us, bully people were doing their various bits for the cause, while the dogs had themselves a rare old time doing what bullies love best - absorbing attention, tidbits, and the fun of the day. What a wonderful occasion this is and I can't tell you how proud I am to be able to take part in it.

This time, just this once, one of those awful luvvy speeches of undying gratitude would actually be genuine. Shall I do one, then? (Ouch! Apparently 'not'.) Maybe this is what celebs mean when they say that fame can go to your head?

# Useless

## A fine display of utter purposelessness...

This cat does mega–poos.

Morris is useless. He really is you know. He's utterly, totally, unavoidably and Olympically devoid of any practical purpose whatsoever. Yes, I know he's not supposed to be a handy addition to the household, and he's the ultimate when it comes to dispensing affection, loyalty, methane and slobber, but surely it's not too much to expect him to occasionally help out, is it? Apparently, it is too much. He's stupendously pointless in every practical way.

Example. As reported a few traumas ago, we now have one of those designer-type gardens. Previously, thanks to Morris's attempts to visit the earth's core, we had a tank training ground. Now, all has been membraned, slabbed , mulched and water featured into a glorious confection of low-maintenance sterility. Morris is not allowed to set an unaccompanied foot in that garden and Herself even scolds the sparrows for poo'ing on the bird bath. Sparrows may not be as common as they once were, but Herself reckons their behavior couldn't be more so. I can hear her 'tutting' from my office, as she restores the bird bath to operating theatre hygiene via a barrage of antiseptic wipes. Anyway, you get the picture.

Now introduce to that picture if you will, next-door's rancid cat. This thing is the Surrey puma. It's the size of a labrador, dumps like a carthorse and regards our splendid expanse of granite chippings as the mother of all litter boxes. This is not a good thing, and, obviously, it must be entirely my fault because that's what I'm for. Truth to tell, it wouldn't be difficult for Morris to repel that cat. You see, it's one seriously freaked-out feline and runs several miles if so much as spoken to harshly. Should Morris ever deign to bark at the thing it'll go into orbit and leave most of its lives behind. That's all I'm asking, see?

Other dogs would defend their territory with pride, passion or at least the odd bark. Not Morris. He simply lies there as the puma launches itself at our fence with an ear-shattering clatter of fat cat on panelling, watches it haul its poo-laden self up the trellis, onto the shed roof and into the garden, where it sneers at Morris as it enjoys a leisurely dump in our granite chippings. Due to the stickiness of what's deposited, I lose half a sack of chippings every time I clean up after that cat and its spectacular bowels, not to mention the time I spend re-raking so Herself won't notice and throw a fit. Which she never fails to. I'm told that the screams (mostly mine) can be heard on the M25. All entirely avoidable, if only Morris would make himself useful for a nano-second.

I know he notices the cat, because his ears flick round when it slams into our fence and his eyes follow it from the entry into our garden, to the exit of the dump. Between these events Morris even has the nerve to look over at me as if to say, 'Well, aren't you going to do something about that?' It's all right for him, though. He's got a kennel to hide in when Herself's radar detects yet another Kit-e-Kat landmine nestling amongst the granite.

I don't want Morris to be hair-trigger yappy and explode into convulsions of barking every time an earwig trundles across the patio. Neither do I wish him to strut, stiff-legged and full of foreboding, around the perimeter of my property until he wears away a patrol trench with his purposeful paws. All I want is for him to tell that scabby cat to sod off and unload its bum-bay somewhere else. This is all very frustrating, you know.

Naturally, being the analytical writer-bloke that I am, I've sussed the whole psychology deal behind Morris's attitude to that cat. You see, like every other problem in this world this one stems from a lack of self-esteem. It's true because I've seen it on the telly. Some toerag mugs a pensioner and on comes Dr. Justin Fyne-Myjob to tell us that the toerag's act was not some malicious manifestation of laziness and lack of respect, but a cry for help due to low self-esteem. And that's exactly what's going on with the cat that craps in my garden.

It knows it's just a turd-delivering trespasser and it hates itself for it. Consequently, it hates the rest of the world, including Morris. That's why it sneers at him like it does. Morris, being the friendly old soul that he is – remember, he once adopted a family of hedgehogs causing a flea infestation of Herself's Axminster - he knows that the cat has enough on its plate as it is, without being bullied by a bull terrier. He's very intuitive, is Morris.

Sadly, he's also absolutely bloody useless.

# Trances With Wolves

## Where wolf?...

He can trance in sweet peas, too.

Morris has recently called all three of his brain cells into a meeting and, between them, they've decided that it's time he went back to his roots. Therefore, he has been reverting to wolf-status all over the house. How convenient that is, in new-millennium Surrey.

Like all allegedly domesticated dogs, Morris displays the odd trait of wildness here and there. Sadly, most are displayed 'here', rather than the vastly more convenient 'there', but with Morris it was ever thus. He doesn't do convenient; never has, never will. Instead, he does, 'Oh my God! Look what he's bloody-well done now!' When, wolfishly, he gorges on his latest caribou carcass (mega-bowl of Supa Dog Ultimate, with added unhealthy treats on top) then, before the local grizzly bears can rob him of his hard-earned kill, he scoots off to up-chuck and re-scoff it at his leisure behind our sofa - he's only doing what comes naturally.

Same goes with scent-marking. When Morris strolls past the kitchen radiator, a landmark representing the extreme southern perimeter of his territory, he absolutely has to cock his leg and give it a tinkle. For if he's less than thorough about his boundary marking, some wolfie-come-lately from a neighbouring pack might well fancy his chances of staking a claim to Morris's house. Obviously. Well it is to him, so don't poke fun.

For maximum effect and minimal wastage of stinky deposits, a wild dog's scent should to be spread far and wide. Like most lusty lobos, Morris broadcasts his butch aroma by raking backwards with his feet after a good wee, to scoot any scent-carrying topsoil he can muster, toward the horizon. Only Morris does it after most dumps, as well as apre-widdle, which is nice. As proven before dozens of witnesses at this year's Bull Terrier Club fund raiser, Morris's scent-spreading abilities can produce divots that Tiger Woods and co. could scarcely comprehend. During the picnic-in-the-orchard phase of the fundraiser, he hurled a fine selection of rearward clods over anyone within scenting distance - which was an impressive five yards as I recall.

Lately, Morris's regression to wolfhood has taken the form of circling three times before flopping down in front of 'his' radiator, or 'his' fire, or 'his' fan-heater that's the only source of hyperthermia-avoidence in my office, thank-you very much. I've seen a million dogs do this. They perform a discrete pirouette before curling nose to tail and taking their ease. Not Morris. He attacks the maneuver in the manner of a discus thrower, by winding himself up, charging his fat bod with centrifugal force and hurling it into whatever it is he's only supposed to be lying in front of.

When such a reckless method of repose is inflicted on my fan-heater, it skitters across the tiled floor, leaving Morris a yard from his original target. The whole routine is then re-enacted, producing an identical result, and around we go again until the fan-heater becomes trapped against something solid, or Morris can't be bothered to keep being a wolf and goes to kip wherever he's crashed.

The latest wild manifestation may have nothing at all to do with being a wolf, but it's certainly not something I've taught him, that's for sure. Morris has taken to trancing. He is a Morris trancer - sorry, couldn't resist it. Yes, I know that this phenomenon is well documented among bull terriers and all manner of theories, conclusions and snotty rows have broken out about it among their owners, but it's only just started happening round our house, so forgive my fascination.

Morris trances with his head poked into the ivy which holds up the walls of our back garden. He just waddles up, sticks his head into the variegated tangle of green and white leaves, and becomes a statue for up to half an hour. Except for his tail, which vibrates, ever so slightly at the very tip. I never disturb him when he's trancing, in fact I only wish he'd do more of it. Seven hours a day would be handy. Morris is an angel when he's trancing.

At trance's end, Morris pulls his bonce out of the ivy, has a quick shake and a couple of yawns, then he's back in his real world of inspired mayhem once more. He farts a lot after trancing, too, I've noticed. Perhaps the trembling of his tail is caused by internal upheaval, as his hypnotised bowels struggle to contain their seething mass of semi-digested Supa Dog Ultimate, with added unhealthy treats. Beats me. What say the trance-experts among the readership?

So, that's Morris regressing, then. It can be but a matter of time before he starts howling at the moon. He may well discover that he enjoys that particular facet of wolfhood even more than trancing. Howling's very therapeutic, when the stresses of canine behavior become too much for this modern world to cope with. I'm an expert on it, I am. I've been howling at the moon for ages. Since...er...not long after Morris arrived, to be exact.

# Foam Pest

## In which Morris tries to drown me...

Well, Morris has had a fine old time lately. First he tries to murder me, and then convinces me that he's contracted a terminal illness. Not bad for a thick Bull Terrier in a slow week in Surrey.

The murder attempt came about because Morris and I share a bathroom. Obviously, we don't actually take turns with the mouthwash and cotton buds. Morris just whines and squeaks hysterically if I don't let him into the bathroom when it's finally my turn to wallow in the grey, gritty dregs left over after Herself and our three fine sons have steeped their carcases for an hour - each. For once, though, I'd got to the bath ahead of the pack and was determined to soak myself into prunehood while reading about hummingbirds and soil erosion, all courtesy of an ancient edition of National Geographic. Morris, as usual, plonked his front paws over the edge of the bath and watched adoringly as my body absorbed Radox, and my mind tried to do the same with Himalayan revelations. So far, so super.

Strangely, the high-speed shenanigans of hummingbird society failed to hold my interest, and I lobbed the mag aside to submerge as much of my body as possible. Being a 6ft 4in sort of guy, with more padding than your average Chesterfield sofa, total submersion is a bit of an acquired art. I have to slide my head down until nostrils meet soap suds, then my displaced feet can lodge themselves either side of the taps. Optimum soakage is then controlled by careful breathing while I bob gently in the soothing swell.

Morris has seen this ritual billions of times and apart from the occasional 'Oi, I'm still here, you know', sort of whimper, he just grazes on the bubbles until I'm sufficiently marinaded to rejoin the world. I can only guess that Morris must have lost sight of me behind a drifting mass of herbal suds and thus, it was pure concern for my safety that caused him to leap astride my chest and bark furiously as we both sank with half a gallon of designer bathwater in my lungs.

He chose the precise moment when my eyes had all but closed and the sacred bath trance was just about to descend. What descended instead was dopey bloody Morris, who stomped on my chest, stomach, and all sorts of other things completely undesigned for stomping on. Upon surfacing, I roared, coughed and ejected at least enough slimy water from my chest cavity to exchange drowning for traditional breathing. When speech became possible, I shouted at the barking mutt, "Yooosstooopidsoddingbloodyhopelessdogyou bloodynearlykilledme!!!"

The effort of this outburst loosened another bucketful of bath water from my respiratory system, which exited via my nose and had me bent over the sink until I stopped retching. Call me harsh, but I think Morris got off lightly, considering I was burping Radox for a week. He thought he'd been crucified though and did that slitty-eyed 'Oh, pardon me for existing' look that every Bull Terrier owner must learn to ignore.

As if this wasn't enough, Morris decided to worry the life out me. I was walking him in his comfy new collar, which was wider than the one he'd recently chewed into oblivion, and was thinking how splendid he looked. Then, for no reason at all, Morris developed a funny walk except it wasn't funny at all. Every 100 yards or so, he'd lose the use of his back leg and would do a little breakdance. I'd already resigned myself to the fact he'd either eaten a kilo of strychnine or that a flat-out stroke was only a leg twitch away.

Mercifully, Morris made it through the night without further trauma until I took him for his next walk. Same thing again. Walk, shuffle, skip-twitch, walk. I was devastated, not to mention racked with guilt for shouting at him over hardly murdering me at all. On reaching home, Morris again recovered while I worried myself sick over what the hell could be afflicting him. Well, it's too late to cut a long story short, but you'll never guess what Morris's tragic illness was. His 'divvy spot'. Every dog has one. If you scratch it, the dog's legs switch to auto-pilot and jump around. Of course, the collar came off when we got home and with it went the stroke-cum-poisoning symptoms. Someone once told me that owning a dog is a great way to relax. Whoever made Morris couldn't read the instructions properly.

# Shoe Fox Shoo!

## Just what I need – another four-footed felon...

Shouldn't these come in pairs?

You know how you allocate a sort of mental budget to cope with the future problems of life? It's that cerebral provision which helps us cope with unavoidable hassles, like our childrens' costs of living, the decline of our bodily functions and the escalation of trial-by-fireworks every time some wannabe achieves its 30th birthday and includes us in yet another bloody midnight percussion-fest. Anyway, pet-hates aside, we all stash a little concern for the trials of life, but I bet that none of you ever imagined that one of those concerns would involve a fox burgling your house and knicking your kids' shoes.

Come on, admit it. You didn't see that one coming, did you? I know I didn't. It's happening, though. Oh yes. We are currently the victims of a fox with a shoe fetish. I say again - it's just not an issue any normal family expects to have on the agenda, is it?

Foxy's M.O. is basic but effective. At any time between midnight and dawn, he (I've been close enough to him to know he's a 'he', too) trots down our road, hangs a left into our modest drive, triggers the security light, ignors it completely, then mooches into our porch, grabs a shoe and offwardly sods with it. Parents among the readership will be aware that the shoes of the modern youngster are not cheap things. In fact, it's the rules that juvenile shoes must *never* be cheap, due to the shame of wearing anything that costs less than a week's rent in Belgravia. This rule applies especially to trainers. Those very trainers that will be kicked off at the door and left there, vulnerable to urban fox attack because, in our house at least, it's also compulsory to leave the porch door open.

To date, we've been foxed out of three trainers (singular, but no cheaper to replace) and a ludicrously expensive loafer. Now steady yourself for the bill. Ready? That'll be the very thick end of three-hundred quid please. You read it right - that's a three, followed by a hat-trick of noughts. Admittedly, all four items were purchased courtesy of various 'never to be repeated' sales, which by a glorious stroke of luck seem to happen on a regular basis. Sadly, all of the stolen brands seem to have been dropped from the discounted line-ups, thus the full RRPs hoik the damage to £300.

So much expense, yet no mention of Morris? How can this be? Easy, it can't be. Morris had his chance at glory and failed. In fact, I'm not so sure that Morris isn't the Mr. Big in this entire scam. Herself is convinced he's done a deal with the fox to deflect attention from his own multi-misdemeanors and the fox is just his fall-guy. It could be argued that exposure to Morris has prejudiced Herself's take on things, but he's a tough client to defend at the best of times - and Morris rarely allows those sorts of times to happen.

We were three shoes into the great fox rip-off, when I gave Morris his chance to do something constructive for the family. His run adjoins the invaded porch, therefore he would adopt the role of Foxscarer General and rid us of the one-beast plague. "We already have a one-beast plague living with us, said Herself, "we will not be supporting another." It's the sheer finality of her statements which causes the shudders, bolstered by the set of her apres-statement mouth and the blinding arc-spark of her eyes striking mine. Thus it was that one balmy night Morris found himself on guard duty.

Morris's stint as our Securicor officer was never designed to be the most arduous task attempted by dog-kind. He had a choice of beds, both duvet'd, with one an in-kennel arrangement while the other offered al-fresco freedom to enjoy the stars, smells and sounds of his night shift. He had refreshments aplenty, no pressure to succeed due to our permanent nil expectation of success and but a single job, i.e. to scare the bejazuz out of the ginger Raffles. A bark would do, or even a forceful thrust of body language, anything which would make foxy realise that our gaff ain't no soft touch no more.

Morris failed. Utterly, completely, non-negotiably, irretrievably failed. Alerted by the security light bathing our bedroom at 3 a.m., I watched through a curtain-chink as Morris the Securicorpse simply lay on his bed and watched foxy pull off yet another blag. Perhaps I could forgive my pointless pet if he'd been sleeping throughout this raid, but that excuse was nullified by the cock of his ear and the twitch of his tail as wild Surrey's version of Imelda Marcos did a runner with the ludicrous loafer. Bark? Deter? Defend? Morris didn't even get up. In fact he was asleep again before the security light that had so rudely awakened him had switched itself off.

I eventually solved the fox problem (so far at least) by lobbing a water-filled balloon on top of the little ginger git during his attempt to filch a shoe I'd cleverly tied down outside the porch. Foxy hated that and hasn't been back since, despite our sons continuing to leave plenty of designer bait in the porch and Herself continuing to refuse to pick it up after them

Morris, meanwhile, remains oblivious. He does 'oblivious' really well. None finer, in fact. It's a gift which has got him where he is today. Morris has a life of luxury, fan mail, no responsibilities and all he can eat, drink, chew and widdle over. There are times, my friends, when I really wish I was in Morris's shoes.

# Morris Goes O.T.T.

## Morris finds the gateway to freedom...

The day began like any other; the kids were surly, no-one could find their socks, reams of important homework hadn't been done, Herself was refusing to write fictitious excuse-notes to cover teenage laziness, Morris had been ordered to his outside kennelly-bit to gorge, vomit, then re-scoff his breakfast and I had manfully ducked-out of it all and gone to the office early. As always, our three boys and their half-done homework were eventually stuffed into Herself's car and, mere minutes later, ejected near a handy school. Having eaten his breakfast at least twice, Morris now waddles into his carpeted kennel for his morning nap, leaving Herself to endure a two-hour retail therapy session in a Kingston megastore or two. Just another day in Doe'sville.

With credit cards wilting, Herself returned to our house to find that we were one item down in the unfeasibly thick bull terrier department. Morris had gone. Run away. Perhaps even stolen. She phoned me immediately. "Erm...I don't suppose you've got Morris with you...at all?" she said. "Oh yes", I said, "I popped back home and picked him up so's he could answer a few e-mails for me. Now what's going on?"

What was 'going on' was that Morris had demolished the gate at the side of our house. This sturdy, hardwood partition had withstood his attentions for quite a while, but for reasons beyond the grasp of mortal man, Morris had decided that morning to lay waste to the gate - and he laid just enough waste to allow him to wriggle through and escape into the unsuspecting world, en-route for our friendly neighbourhood convenience store.

Morris likes this shop and he's taken there on a regular basis, so even he can remember the way. With no handler to restrict access, Morris marched into the store like he owned the place, and began a shoplifting spree comprising two packets of mint Yo-Yos and a Toblerone. Understandably, the shop manager called the police, who then called in the experts from the Old Windsor branch of the Battersea Dogs Home, who came out and apprehended the culprit. Thus ended Morris's life of crime approximately 30 minutes after it had begun.

Of course, I didn't know any of this and immediately assumed that my wee pet was now ducking between trucks on the M25, or pounding out the miles on a treadmill after being pumped full of steroids by some maniac dog-fighter moron. Everything was my fault and I gave myself an almighty shellacking. How many times had I intended to get Morris microchipped? Why didn't I build that gate out of tungsten? And why on God's earth did I ever choose a dog with the destructive capability of a platoon of sappers coupled to the brain of a small radish?

I hit the phone at a run, drawing a discouraging blank at all police stations within 20 miles, plus the R.S.P.C.A. and the dog warden of our local council. After listening to my detailed description of Morris - 'pure white bull terrier, no, not a staff', the one with the slitty eyes and egg-shaped head, with brindle ears and fluorescent pink testicles. Yes, that means he's a male, yes' - one police station desk-person asked me if I was sure that Morris wasn't a black and white border collie, because they'd definitely had one of those handed in.

My faith in the legal system was restored when the council offices called me back to confirm that Morris was safely in custody. Whilst my blood pressure normalised, the council-lady explained that, for a mere 50-quid, I could collect a release voucher from her office, after which I would be permitted to get my dog out of nick. With relief flooding out of me and drenching everything from armpit to underpant, I dived into my car and headed for the council offices. The lady manning the Irresponsible Dog Owners counter told me that Morris had 'been a bit of a naughty boy while he was out', prompting fresh visions of mayhem and catastrophe in my already over-adrenalised brain.

As it turned out, she was only recounting Morris's confectionary-blagging exploits in the shop, so with thanks and apologies trailing behind me, I paid up, grabbed my dog's get-out-of-jail-expensively card and lit out for Battersea Old Windsor. I'd been to this place before when looking for a mate for Morris ( sadly, we couldn't find anything that could be expected to tolerate him) but I could hardly believe my eyes when I drove into the car park to find a sparkly new building, inside which was a fantastic dog and can re-homing facility.

What a wonderful place this is, complete with pet accessories store and the most helpful staff on the planet. Morris had been inoculated and flea-treated as a matter of policy, and he'd also been given the most suitable name of 'OTT'. Oh yes, within minutes of arriving at Battersea Old Windsor, my dog had been awarded the label which sums up his approach to life, the universe and everything in it - Over The Top. I was charged £7.20 for his jab and anti-flea job, which was far too reasonable, so I made a donation, thanked the staff once more and took Morris back to the home he so loves to eat bits of.

A new gate will cost £200 to make, I'd done 50-quid on bail-money, plus a few more to Battersea Old Windsor for their superb care of 'OTT', I still had to grovel to the owner of the shop Morris had pillaged and I'd flirted with a coronary for a minute or two. As I said at the start - just a day like any other.

# Mourning Sickness

## Meet the world's most enthusiastic bereavement councelor...

We appear to have moved home. Our address now reads, The House of Drear, Melancholy Mansions, Mournville. Children are wailing, the produce of the new - and uncomfortably roguish - Captain Birdseye, are prodded around teatime plates before being ignored, and even the sacred weekly ritual of watching Buffy The Vampire Slayer on Sky One was passed over out of respect for the dear departed. For dear readers, and I know many of you have shared the grief that afflicts us now, because...the bloody hamster has died.

Yes folks, 'Linford' has stuffed his cheek-pouches with celestial sunflower seeds and shuffled his dumpy little bum off to hamster heaven. It's a sad loss and obviously the media will have to be alerted, but I thought I'd let you lot know first.

As anyone who has kept them will know, God only invented hamsters to train youngsters in the art of trauma management. These little time-bombs of grief are designed to exist just long enough to become part of the junior consciousness, then to expire in a twitch of a heartrending whisker - bringing even the hulking pre-teen to its knees in shuddering sobs of remorse. Having laid out Linford in his taped-up toilet roll insert coffin, I also noticed that hamsters somehow contrive to look even cuter when they're dead. This is to make me feel guilty for all the times I tied up its wheel to stop the incessant racket of Linford's nocturnal training runs.

Morris, being a big and hairy, white-with-pink-testicles sort of a bull terrier, is neither as cute or as intelligent as a hamster but he's totally tuned to the family vibe and soon sussed that spirits were flagging after Linford's sad demise. 'Nature abhors a vacuum' someone once said, and because like all rational males, I too despise the Hoover, I was pleased to see my Morris step in to fill the Linford void.

Morris isn't an arm round the shoulder sort of guy, he's more of a diversion'ist. Thus, when we find ourselves in times of sorrow Mother Morris comes to us - speaking fluent moron - let it be, eee. What Morris decides on as the most therapeutic diversions for the family, are not always what the family would prescribe for itself but there's no denying that his antics do take your mind off things.

This time, Morris began the healing process by carting my youngest son's schoolbag off to his kennel and chewing the handles off. Normally, Stephen would have thrown his well-practised wobbly and stomped around the house vowing never to go to school until a proper bag was supplied, 'And not the Thomas The stinky Tank Engine one, Mum - I am nine years old you know!' Yet this time he seemed resigned to the bag's destruction, perhaps because his soul had been wrung dry of emotion through hamster grief, but more likely that the logo on the bag just wasn't cutting on the streets any more, and something way-cooler was required anyway.

Morris then supplied succour to our eldest by forcibly diverting him from morning walkies and towing him into the garden of a girlie down the road, who my lad definitely fancies but he won't admit it. Said girly's family own a brace of boxers who Morris romps with in the park, and they were slobbering over the side-gate entrance to girly's garden. Morris put himself into four-wheel drive mode, where resistance is futile, and dragged Kristopher gatewards. The resulting festival of creative barking and gate-rattling brought girly's angry dad running to investigate, followed by, oh no, her girlyship in person!

Kristopher was mortified to be spotted by his fancy-bit while failing to disentangle Morris's head from the bars of the gate and being told off by her dad at the same time. I mean, Kristopher hadn't moussed his hair or anything and he was wearing naff trainers. Oh God dad, he's never going out again - apparently.

Obviously Morris couldn't conclude his treatment without ministering to Herself. So he snuck into our bedroom and scoffed 2 lbs. of hand-made Belgian chocolates I'd bought her as a brownie-points gathering exercise, in lieu of an upcoming fishing trip. Showing remarkably good taste for one who regularly raids the dustbin for used teabags, Morris chose to spit out the coffee-flavoured choccies, although things would have been a tad less noisy had he chosen to hawk them up on anything but Herself's dressing table seat.

One way and another, with Morris's peculiar brand of consolation to guide us through the bad times, I know we'll get over the tragic loss of Linford. Just to make sure though, I took the precaution of burying Linford's bog-roll sarcophagus in the far corner of our garden, well away from Morris's open-cast mining area. What we don't need right now is a mud-caked Morris bounding into the lounge, the mummified Linford dangling from his chops, for an impromptu re-creation of Stephen King's Pet Cemetery. R.I.P. Linford - at least I bloody well hope so.

# Dripping The Light Fan-Tastic!

## It's getting hot in here...

Not my fan –
Morris's. I don't
actually have a
fan. Morris does
and this is it. Not
that I go on about
it or anything...

Morris has a new fan. No, not another discerning person that sends him letters without so much as mentioning me thanks very much (you lot know who you are, and there's plenty of you, but I'm waaay too classy to even mention the cruel injustice of it all) I'm talking about a pluggy-in-type fan. It's to cool him down to combat the strain of doing sod-all for hours on end, while I work myself into a foam to keep Morris supplied with luxuries, like fans.

Herself bought the fan for him during the summer that'll be all but over by the time you get to read this. Herself hardly seems to hate Morris at all these days, and he certainly gets more treats than I do. Most odd, I trust you'll agree. This new fan sits on my office desk and it's pointed at Morris's bed. That's 'permanently pointed', rather than wafting from side-to-side in a way that would cool me down a bit, too.

How many fans do you think I've got. That'll be none then. Of any sort, as it happens. Oh don't worry about me, I'm only the poor sap who slaves away at this melting keyboard so the rest of the family, including its hairiest, least-contributing, most-troublesome, Morris-shaped member, can enjoy life to the full. Some alpha male I've turned out to be.

The excuses for my being deprived of a personal fan are, frankly, pathetic. Herself had the cheek to tell me that I can't have a fan blowing on me as I write because my desk is so bloody messy that papers and stuff would fly everywhere and she knows that I wouldn't clear it all up when it landed on the floor. As if.

She compounded this nonsense by declaring that if I'd sort out the rubbish and file it all away like a normal person would, I could have any amount of fans. I explained, with commendable patience I must say, that we artistic types cannot flourish in a sterile environment. We need a little thought-provoking chaos around us, to remind us that we're all daring and edgy and all that. Herself said that I didn't look daring, just sweaty and grumpy. Then she made some non-witty comment about me obviously being a hot-house flower, and stalked off to the fan-assisted living room to watch something on telly that had police sirens in it. Ten seconds later, she came back, switched on Morris's fan, scowled threateningly at me, and really left. Obviously, I rule.

Here's the kicker. When I'm wilting away in my office – and somehow managing to avoid being even slightly resentful of Morris and his personal fan - not only do I get zilch by way of cooling breezes, I get to enjoy my dog's re-circulated farts. This ensures that every one of these creeping assassins is appreciated to the full, with at least four curtain calls per emission. One of nature's few concessions to me, is the fact that some of Morris's farts are heavier than air and sink to the floor to die, rather than rearing-up and grabbing me by the throat. Morris's fan ends that concession. It gives his farts wings and allows them to soar into the Terryosphere, where they explode like sulphurous fireworks and sting my eyes.

So picture if you will, the summer version of poor me. There I hunch, broiling quietly, vainly trying to please some distant editor with my keyboard-pokings, whilst suffering the death of a thousand wafts. Regular readers will know that I'm not one to exaggerate, or indeed queen it up a bit to inspire sympathy. In fact, my version is pretty much guaranteed to be underplayed to a quite noble degree. Are you touched? Me too, according to Herself.

Right, I've got to mention the book. No, I really have to give it a plug, it's in my contract. Probably. Anyway, due to the Dogs Today time-lag, caused mainly by the editorial team lounging around on velvet cushions and drinking Lambrini when they should be working, by the time you get to read this you'll have already seen what a sure-fire, can't-miss, must-have bargain 'A Guide Dog For The Thick' represents.

It's got dozens of Morris stories in it, plus loads of photos, a full colour, A5 format that's ideal for reading in the loo or taking on holiday or foisting on friends and family as a Christmas present – and it's only £9.99. Come on, you've just seen how I suffer for my art. The least you could do is to reward me lavishly. In fact, if enough of you buy my book, I'll be able to get one of those portable air-conditioning jobbies that can be trundled to wherever they're needed. Ooh yes, now that will outrank Morris's silly fan and no mistake. Mind you, with my luck Herself will see that I'd won and, just to wind me up, she'd buy Morris his own swimming pool or something. As I say, I'm not one to exaggerate...

# Break From Tradition

## Looks like it's all my fault, then...

Bless! Living proof that ignorance is bliss.

A huge and significant realisation has been lately forced upon me. I am now required to think the unthinkable, and, if that little impossibility wasn't impossible enough - I may well have to apologise, too.

So, who do I have to apologise to, then? Morris, that's who. And what is this revelation wot hath come unto me all biblical stylie? Oh, only that Morris's disastrous life may not be his fault at all. That he could very possibly not be the architect of mayhem, as defined, portrayed and broadcast by yours truly, and that some other misadventure-magnet could have been the catalyst for the calamities which have dogged our lives. You see, the only other presence consistent with Morris's misadventures is (gulp) me.

When bully-bedlam breaks out, I'm always there. To whom did Morris lead that enraged bull? Who was the only conscious adult present when Morris filled his bed with hedgehogs and the house with fleas? Who was attached to Morris when he walked off the bridge? And, in front of an awed public, who was it who stooged for Morris at the Welfare fund-raiser, as he poo'd in the show ring, peed in a lady's handbag, widdled in his water bowl and drank it, then hurled clods of turf at peaceful picnic'ers? Me, me, and a thousand other times, me.

# A Guide Dog For The Thick

Here's where my unthinkable theory really takes shape. Two months ago, with not a hint of Morris within 10 miles of me, I fell into a hole and broke my arm. It wasn't badly broken. It was incredibly well-broken, actually, with all manner of unfeasible flourishes to its credit. OK, no big deal, and these things happen. But, and I swear that not a syllable of what I'm about to recount has been artistically licensed in any way, what followed the break proved beyond doubt that I am marked by fate as a repository for un-happened catastrophes.

Try not to become too upset on my behalf, impossible though it may well be. Instead, consider the odds of this lot happening to a normal, non-cursed person;

There I am, lying horizontal in a hole, in a field, in a foot of stinky water, my left arm having been turned into an anatomically incorrect bendy-toy and swelling grotesquely by the second. I spot salvation in the form of a nearby angler, who had seen me disappear from the landscape and was now off his foldy chair and peering at me as I extricated myself from the hole. I wave the angler over, he waves cheerily back. I shout 'HELLOOO-AAH! CAN YOU HELP ME?' He waves again, takes to his chair once more and settles back to read his copy of What Maggot? Monthly.

What the....? I re-shout, re-wave and regain my feet, swaying in the knowledge that I was about to throw up and/or swoon like a total wuss. Either way, I could have done with a wee bit of assistance and my oblivious angler was my only source. For ten minutes, too unsteady to walk toward him and between spasms of pain and puking, I screamed and waved at the angler like a monosyllabic semaphore enthusiast. Eventually, he looked up, did a pantomime double-take at my gibbon dance of desperation, and came to my aid as fast as he could run.

It turned out that my 'reluctant' rescuer was, in fact, profoundly deaf. I was too busy being profoundly grateful to think of the role my calamity curse had assumed in all of this, contenting myself with the use of my savior's mobile phone to summon Herself to meet me at the nearest road, en-route to a rapid NHS glue-and-screw job, with plaster cast novelty gift thrown in. Little did I know that, for me, 'NHS' stood for Now He'll Suffer.

First, they tried to set my arm using gas-and-air, which would have been just about tolerable, had they actually connected the bloody gas. As it was, I was sucking like a madman on a mouthpiece joined to no more than an un-plugged pipe and limitless supplies of plaster room atmosphere. Gosh how they giggled when that teensy mistake was discovered.

They asked if I'd mind spending the night in the plaster room, on account of there being no ward space. I said, 'fine, but get me a bed, please, because this trolley's a foot too short, my legs are getting pins and needles through overhanging the end of it, and deep-vein thrombosis is rather too trendy right now.' They said I could have a bed when a porter could be found. Meekly, I pointed to a bed just 6 feet away, parked with a load more, right outside the plaster room. They told me that only porters are allowed to move beds. I waited 9 hours for a porter to move that bed 6 feet to the right. It was beginning to occur to me, that this wasn't my lucky day. I also realised that Morris was, for the first time, utterly blameless.

Still the disasters flowed. I'll not distress you all with my multiple traumas, but among the lowlights, my broken bones didn't join properly, a re-break was scheduled, delayed, then canceled, and I was left 'nil by mouth' and forgotten for a day when my medical file was 'misplaced'. And someone made me a cup of cold Horlicks. Then, nothing was healing properly and I was found to have something called Sudek's Syndrome, which heightens the body's (mine in this case) pain response and leaves the relevant limb feeling like it's permanently plugged into the mains. All of these inflicted without Morris, remember.

Whilst I was in hospital receiving disasters, Morris didn't put a paw wrong. Immediately upon my return, he ate my laxatives. These were required due to the...erm.. 'consolidating' effect a painkiller diet has on one's system. Morris found my jumbo-economy box of Turbo-Purge, or whatever, ate the lot, and was banished to his kennel until matters took their course. Next day, his bowels scoured by the onslaught of industrial-grade senna, Morris re-entered the house, and within minutes had sat on his tail and dislocated it. Then he pulled my office 'phone off my desk and wrecked the handset. Welcome home, Terry. Things have been kinda quiet around here without you!

# Vet Behind The Ears

## How exciting, as we get a new vet...

Depending on how you look at it, here stands every vet's dream—or nightmare.

"Name?"
"Er...Terry. What's yours then my dear?"
"No, I meant the dog."
"Morris".
"Breed?"
"Poodle."
"Pardon?"
"Bull terrier."
"Sex?"
"Just a cup of tea, thanks".

You knew I was going to say that, didn't you? So did the concrete-faced receptionist at the vet's, but where you sort of half-smiled at my boyish banter, she glared at me as though I was tramp-phlegm. Miserable cow she was, and when Morris is your prospective client a miserable cow is something you just cannot be.

Above and beyond any old qualifications in animal mechanics, taking on my dog in any sort of professional capacity demands an industrial strength sense of humour. I'm hard enough to deal with in matters of Morris, Herself is damn near impossible, but truly, the git-hound himself is worth at least a TV series or two. In fact, 'Morris-Level Stress Management' should be the final module in every vet's training, with counseling available to the traumatised.

We had a very posh vet once. I knew he was posh because his car park was always stuffed with Range Rovers that actually had mud on them. He was the first vet ever to cut Morris's toenails and before he did so, he asked if I minded him putting a muzzle on Morris, "because, well, um, you know Mr. Doe, these dogs are so...well...robust, aren't they?" I told him I'd yet to find it necessary to strap Morris's head inside a leather cage and that I'd rather hold him in a firm but caring grip, but if he really felt so intimidated by Morris then I'd permit a brief muzzling. The posh vet got decidedly snotty at this point and reached into his muzzle locker for the correct bit of dog bondage.

It was while the second securing strap was being cinched tight that Morris awoke from his normal operating mode of dream-state and threw back his head to dislodge the muzzle. The muzzle stayed more or less put, but the posh vet's glasses didn't, and neither did his bottom lip, which split like a freshly trodden slug under the impact of Morris's upwardly mobile skull.

"Good job you put that muzzle on him really. You could've got hurt, you could've". I said, as the posh vet's lip achieved the size of an airbed - and cleverly added at least another £30 to the fee for my cheek. That being his first toenail-clip, Morris didn't behave too badly, in fact he didn't even howl, but boy did I do some fine howling when I got the bill. As I said, we had a very posh vet once.

Our present model is fairly new - fairly new to life itself actually, because he only looks about twelve and Herself even questions the fact that he's a real vet. He must be a vet, though, because he gave me a lift home from the pub a while back and I noticed that his clothes are even less fashionable than mine and his car smells of cat's widdle.

We've not tested him properly because we're between crises right now, although with Morris fresh catastrophes are merely a matter of time. How will he respond, I wonder, to Morris's annual 'oh look everyone - I've rammed another grass seed up my foot', ritual and all of the melodrama that accompanies it. Oh yes, that sorts the vets from the boys, that does.

When Morris absorbs his yearly grass seed the result is bloody scary, at least it is to those of us who haven't seen it all before. That's the test, see. How will Vettus Neuvaux react when Morris The Total Poof hobbles into his surgery with a paw the size, shape and colour of a sun-ripened mango, and starts queening around like a pantomime dame before the vet so much as pokes him up the bum with a moistened thermometer?

Don't think I'm being un-sympathetic to Morris here, please. This is the dog that draped himself across a fan heater and fried his arse without even waking up. Had Herself's bloodhound hooter not detected the stench of Morris's broiling bum, he'd have slept on until chargrilled at least. So I know he puts it on more than a bit when the grass seed performance comes along.

Next time it happens, I'll watch the boy-vet's eyes for signs of trepidation as he weighs up the prospect of a pain-maddened Morris destroying the surgery and its occupants like some canine version of the Incredible Hulk. When the vet extracts that vicious little burrowing seed from the inflamed paw and Morris pretends to faint, will he reach for the resuscitation gear, or will he suss Morris's little game and revive him instantly by putting a chocolate biscuit under his nose, like the old vet used to do? We'll see when his time comes.

One thing's for certain, at least. This latest vet may be young, shiny and new, but he's got a great sense of humour. I met him in the pub again the other night and seeing Morris crashed out and snoring from both ends beneath my stool, he said, "It's a good job all dogs aren't as well behaved as yours, Terry, or I wouldn't have any work to do!" I left him with his naiveté intact, for now. He'll learn soon enough, poor sod.

# Video Nasty

## This time, Morris really takes the ....

Herself went absolutely raving mad when Morris peed on a boxful of these. Understandable, I suppose.

It had been one of those days when life at the office was so brain-meltingly tedious, that I was actually looking forward to coming home and listening to Herself's daily recital about how well the PTA's bloody Christmas bazaar was shaping up.

It's a 'Christmas Craft Fayre actually', I'm usually snootily reminded, ever since the PTA Head Harridan decided the occasion needed an image boost. Oh 'scuse me, beg-pardon moi lady, but drafting in one old hippie who does strange things with candles doesn't turn a bazaar into ye olde traditionale craft fayre - especially when you have 150 kids leaping about on a bouncy castle to the background accompaniment of Bing sodding Crosby singing about children listening for sleigh bells in the snow - neither of which we have in Surrey. Herself is now Vice-Harridan of the PTA and takes her role, as she does most things, extremely fiercely.

She came up with the idea of making a video diary of the outgoing pupil's final year at Our Lady Of Eternal Guilt (a proper junior school, where children and teachers still tremble in the presence of the Headmistress) so the kids can have something to look back and be depressed about in 20 years time when they're fat, grey, bald and mortgaged into adulthood.

Assembling the video footage, having it all edited, interviewing the kiddies on camera, designing the sleeve and sticking a class photo on each, was Herself's only reason to exist for most of the year, and waiting for the finished articles to arrive from the video reproduction company had her in the same state of anxious snarliness as imminent childbirth. Then the great day came when the video-repro man delivered the baby, in the form of a huge open-topped box of superbly turned out tapes.

He put them down for five seconds while Herself signed the delivery note - and er...Morris peed all over them. Oh yes, the whole works - an entire bladderful. Herself had to get her delivery note signing pen from the kitchen, the video man followed her and Morris saw the chance to put his mark on the unguarded crate of tapes. He was just squeezing out the last few drops when Herself caught him, leg raised and bang to rights.

Oh my God. Oh everyone's God. Oh Gods who nobody has ever heard of. Had Morris cocked his leg against a real baby, things would not have been so bad. But those videos were Her absolute baby, and now they had half a gallon of bull terrier widdle over, and in, them. Praise to all those Gods I mentioned before, that I wasn't there when it happened.

The kids told me that when she found out what Morris had done, 'Mum went all funny like that dinosaur in Jurassic Park, sort of roaring in slow motion an' all that'. So it was, that when I came home from my tedious day at the office, I found my house reeking like a tramp's pants with the central heating turned up full blast and every radiator in the house festooned with open video cases.

Herself and the children had gone to McDonalds to escape the stench, and I was left with written instructions.

Dear Terry,
Morris is in his kennel. Please kill him. This time I mean it. Your dinner is in the oven. It will taste of dog piss. For the next year at least, all of your dinners will taste of dog piss, all of your clothes will smell of dog piss and your children will go to school smelling of dog piss, because your dog is not, nor will he ever be, fit to live in civilised company. We now live in The House Of Dog Piss.

Enjoy your dog piss lasagne.

P.S. It's all your fault - and you will pay.

Well that's OK then. Morris lifts his leg, and I get dumped on. 'Twas ever thus as far as I remember.

# (V)et Phone Home

## Phantom illness – real fee...

I've said it before, I'm saying it now, and you can bet any of your favourite organs that I'll be saying it again; Morris isn't like normal dogs. In fact, he isn't even like most bonkers dogs. He's a dog apart. You know that Roswell incident and all of that Area 51 spaceship stuff? Well, that's cobblers. If anyone wants to know what a real alien looks like – it's got piggy eyes, pink testicles and it lives in terrestrial Surrey.

Morris subjects me to out-of-body experiences and abducts money from me on such a regular basis, that I think he's not just an alien, he's some sort of ET Dark Lord or other. Newer readers may imagine that I'm being a bit of an old queen about my dog, even overreacting a fraction. Stalwart Morris followers, though, will be shaking their weary heads and thinking, 'aw Gawd, what's the little sod done this time? Allow me to relate, dear readers.

It all began when I had the nerve to go abroad on a journalistic assignment for a week. Morris doesn't approve of my leaving him and always sulks like a tart from the moment he realizes he's not included in my excess baggage. Morris gets fussed over (which is precisely why he carries on like he does) and I'm forgotten about in minutes. It's a time-honoured system that works every time. This time, though, I lobbed a spanner in those works and Morris responded like the space kidette he truly is.

I requested that, in my absence, Morris should be taken to the vet to have his nails clipped. Yes, it was a cowardly act and I admit that I was copping out of the mayhem that surrounds any nail-clipping carried out at home. Morris hates going to the vets and he loathes having his nails even touched let alone clipped. I knew what I was doing when I put a continent between me and the sub-contracted clipping. What I didn't know, was how far my little alien would go to exact his revenge on me.

I returned from my trip to find Morris the subject of projectile diarrhea. He always throws a bit of a gastro-wobbly after a visit to the vet but this was impressive even by his galactic standards. Vesuvian eruptions of Weetabix coloured poo-lava shot from his bottom in horizontal jets and the sulphur gas which punctuated each blast robbed the very air of oxygen. I don't know what the atmosphere is composed of on Morris's home planet, but it won't support life as we know it, Jim, that's for sure.

# A Guide Dog For The Thick

I began to get concerned when Morris's bum-cano hadn't gone dormant after three days. He'd been on a rice and chicken diet from the first eruption, but still the stinky magma flowed, and he'd now refused to drink. This isn't good. With gallons of outgoing slurry not being replenished by any acceptable fluids, Morris was dehydrating like a houseplant on a sunny windowsill. In common with such plants, he began to wilt before our eyes and I judged it time to risk his hatred of the vet and the panic button was firmly pushed.

By the time I got Morris to the surgery he was off his legs. Well, the front ones worked OK, but a dog as heavy as Morris definitely needs all four. Thus, we staggered into the vet's and the diagnosis began. Truth to tell, I was extremely worried. Morris may act like a total girly when a gnat or ant attacks him, but he shrugs off major trauma like an SAS trooper on steroids. To see him whimper each time his back legs went from under him was like watching my children have their inoculations, and I felt just as useless.

The vet couldn't find anything visibly wrong with Morris, so X-rays were prescribed and he was admitted for 24-hour observation and a complete M.O.T. Anyone who's sat around waiting for a vet to phone will know that each hour takes a fortnight to pass, and how bloody annoying it is when the phone finally rings and it's some git trying to sell you something. I confess I'm a tad short at these times and I can feel the tele-git giving me a two-finger sign off as I hang up on it.

So, 24 hours eventually passed, during which Morris had undergone every test known to man or dog. Guess what? Nothing wrong. Not a thing. Zilcho. In fact the vet was impressed by his general robustness and hearty constitution. The vet was mystified. I wasn't. I knew Morris had performed some sort of alien transmogrification that can't be detected by our backward earthling science. Once Morris had exacted his revenge on me for leaving him, he morphed back into his usual form and could leap tall buildings in a single bound.

Fortunately for the mystified vet – who was professionally fantastic I have to say – the fee of several-hundred-and-fifty quid went some way toward easing the confusion caused by my dog's little jaunt into the diarrhoeasphere. Meanwhile, Morris has won yet again and there's more space in my wallet than there is between his ears. Please beam me up someone. Hello…is there anyone out there?

# A Week's A Long Time...

## The worst dog in the world is back, back, back!

Well, it looks like the one-mutt Armageddon that is Morris is bang in form again. After a couple of relatively dormant months (for which, O Lord we thank thee ) my dog has obviously consulted his 'to-do' diary and caught up on all those little jobs he'd let slip, lately. In a week which has been commendably productive, my dog has, with no help of any kind, achieved the following...

He's toppled the bar-b-que. Quite a feat, and one which has frustrated him in the past, due to my habit of unfairly lashing the bar-b-que to a handy fence post with a triple-wrapped bungee strap. This simple piece of barby-bondage also served to prevent its plastic overcoat thingy from inflating in the wind and taking off to explore the neighbourhood. A great idea and all mine, so I won and Morris lost. Ner, ner, ner-ner ner - and two fingers up to Morris on that one. Oh yes.

Sadly, the structural integrity of bungees is based on rubber and woven string, both of which roll over and die after a mere six months of torrential rain, frosts and regular testing tugs from Morris. Thus, Morris's latest pluck on the bungees yielded a right result, as the perished strands binding the bar-b-que to the fence post went 'pingaty-ping-poinggg' and the barby was free to be towed around our patio on its hopeless plastic wheels and trailing metal legs. The scrape marks reveal that Morris towed it for a distance of exactly six slabs, after which he knocked it over and shredded its cover. That's me already dead, then, and Morris is only just opening his account for the week.

He then ate my niece's posh text book. Casey is a glorious child (she's 18, really, but they're still kids, ay?) and we love her dearly. She's studying to be a children's nurse, or a lion tamer or somesuch fraughtsome career, and she uses my office to write up her work for half an hour, then she spends two hours flirting with boys via e-mail, which she doesn't think I know about. Anyway, Casey left her copy of 'Why Children Are Gits' in my office and Morris decided to make a midnight feast of it. Come cock's crow next morning, Morris was danglies-deep in shredded child-taming techniques and I was looking at a 40-quid bill for a replacement book.

Warmed up nicely, Morris then went for his hat-trick. He stole my best, old jeans, pulled the back pocket off them and ate it. No big deal, this. He usually goes straight for the crutch when he grabs my trouserings, rendering them wearable only in resorts and camps of the type Herself and I have never had the desire or equipment to frequent - if you get my drift. The problem of the scoffed pocket was to re-visit me, however, for my life is neither simple or fair.

Some two hours after he'd eaten the pocket of my jeans, I was in my office writing and watching Morris sprawled out in that 'I've just fallen off the roof' pose of his. Flat on his back, front paws bent and back legs splayed, Morris slept the twitchy sleep of the incurably mischievous, whilst I remained on poo watch throughout the evening. I could stand down as soon as the emergence of a Levi Strauss label could be confirmed. To assist the passage of the pocket, Morris had been double-fed on bulky stuff and had already had me outside in the fading light on three occasions, staring closely at his bottom for the good news. Two widdles and a phantom squat were all I had to report. I'm sure the little sod knew what I was waiting for because he kept drifting towards my office door as if about to ask to go outside, only to turn away as I shifted in my seat to let him out. Then... the retching started.

Morris can retch louder than most dogs can bark and he needs only the tiniest speck of tonsil-tickling detritus around which to build an entire hawking and karking campaign. The pocket of my jeans would provide the catalyst for all manner of eruptions - and indeed it did.

After three, brain-melting hours of Morris's attempts to wretch forth my pocket, he toddled off outside and delivered it via the tradesman's entrance. Probing through the parcel with a stick had me doing a fair imitation of Morris's karking song, but that pocket had to be officially identified. Bless. There it was. All better now.

Nope. Not a chance. On karked Morris for another three hours, between power-kips and attacks of wind that would be instantly banned under the Geneva Convention. By the early hours of the morning I'd fallen asleep at my computer and was well on the way to an advanced case of keyboard face, when the kark to end all karks blasted me into consciousness. This monstrous roaring retch was followed by a metallic 'tinkle', as a tiny shiny object was ejected from Morris's impossibly gaping gob onto the floor tiles of my office. It was a mangled ring-pull, later identified as coming from a can of Pepsi. Where the rest of the can resides, I dread to think. Knowing Morris, he'll probably store the can in his colon until he's built up a decent head of gas, then fire it through our patio doors just for a laugh.

As I said, the lad's on form and there's a whole month's worth of possibility between this column and the next. Heavens, what fun I'll have. Or possibly not.

# And The Banned Played On

Another outbreak of acceptable behavior ends in style...

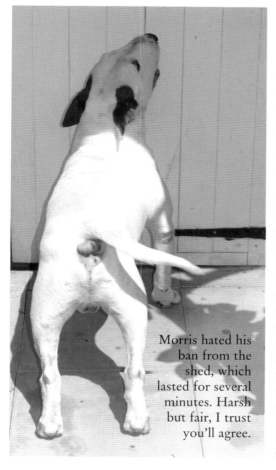

Morris hated his ban from the shed, which lasted for several minutes. Harsh but fair, I trust you'll agree.

It saddens me to report that Morris's recent flash of good behavior was but a blip on the catastrophe catalogue that is his life. At three weeks, nine hours and thirty-several minutes, it was by far the best blip he's managed since records began but as the Rolling Stones sang way back in the Formica-age - 'It's all over now.'

Morris ended his truce with the forces of disaster, in a flurry of totally unacceptable pranks which have resulted in him being banned from just about every square inch of his former territory. No longer can he wander like a waddling wildebeest across the trackless wastes of the back garden. No more may he flatten our petunias with a downward plonk of his puckered pink bum. The most tragic'est thing of all though, is that Morris has been cast down from his little piece of heaven - the blessed shed.

For 'twas in this very shed that Morris first discovered the mouse that he's had a passionate relationship with for the past two years. Now, not being a mouseycologist, I don't know if your average scuttling rodent even lives for two years, but if it's not the same mouse then Morris is certainly none the wiser. Whoever the mouse happens to be at the time, Morris loves it.

Morris will move mountains to get closer to 'his' mouse. For 'mountains' read mower, a tangled stack of mountain bikes (at least it is now) and boxes of girly baby stuff gathered by Herself, which never saw action because I had the good sense to supply her with man-cubs only. "Find me one male human who I could look upon and think, 'Hmmmm, wouldn't it be wonderful if he seduced my daughter and we'll have us one of those girl-type babies." I'd trot this out when my fear of producing anything that wasn't boy shaped entered the conversation. End of conversation. Beginning of scowly sulk.

But like Morris's acceptable behavior blip, that baby-having stuff's all over now, Herself and I have had our litter, they were all boys as the Good Lord intended, and there'll be no more breeding for us. Apart from the odd accidental hamster.

Back to Morris and the mouse. It, or a new version of it, must have reappeared, and Morris must have spent the entire day and half the night in the shed heaving aside obstructions in his desire to get next to it. When I went to claim him at bedtime, I could hear him in the shed whining like a puppy. When bull terriers whine, it's because they want something. When they want something, if you're not there to stop them, they'll find some way of getting it - usually a particularly expensive way if my experience is anything to go by.

Morris's chosen way consisted of, 'drag the mower away from the mousehole by ripping it out by its power cable, then weave the family bicycles into metallic spaghetti and garnish with a scattering of unused baby-gear sauce.' Morris was about to start prizing up the floorboards when I poked him up the nuts with a garden cane.

So that's it, he's banned from the shed. He got himself banned from the garden because he demolished the rockery and left Herself's cherished alpines lying flat on their backs with their roots in the air, until the sun fried them all up. A sudden shower turned what was left of our rockery, into a muddery, and Morris's garden ban has been extended indefinitely.

But does he care? Care is it? I doubt if he even knows. Give him me to annoy, something chewy and challenging to demolish and his daily lorry load of gas-producing grub, and he's as delirious as ever. Obviously I tell Herself that he's suffering the death of a thousand cuts and that her punishment regime is really teaching him the error of his ways.

Some chance. This is the dog that licks electrified cattle fences for a laugh. What's the odds of a bit of territorial deprivation having any sort of effect on Morris - the hairy embodiment of 'ignorance is bliss?' There's about as much chance of Morris mending his ways, as there is of him mending the lawnmower.

# To Blazes With It!

## Gunpowder, treason and...plop

Well, it'll soon be bonfire month. I'm sure I remember when a single night was all we needed to celebrate the non-blowing-up of Parliament via colourful explosions all over the place. Now, Guy Fawkes 'night' begins half-way through October and wrecks most of November before it blows itself out. I know I'm getting old - because I dread it.

Morris hates it too, you know. Oh yes. Strangely, despite my detailed explanation of what Guido and co failed to do a few centuries ago, and why it's still so desperately significant (yeah-right) Morris still fails to grasp why we set fire to millions of quids' worth of decorative violence every year. I'm sure he also joins me in wondering why, if we must go pyro-technically potty for weeks on end, the bloody fireworks are getting louder instead of prettier.

We are not alone in our dread of November the 5th - not by a long chalk. Only the other day I was talking to Mrs. Thingy from the houses behind where the Co-Op used to be, and she loathes bonfire season even more than I do. It's her cats, see? They react to fireworks in a most worrying fashion, scooting up the curtains and wedging themselves behind the nearest pelmet at the first up-chuck from a Roman candle. Morris whimpers, shifts uneasily about and occasionally barks his empty head off, but he's yet to scale the drapes. Heaven forbid.

Mrs. Thingy's cats won't come down for hours, either, and when they do, it's only to poo and widdle in Axminster'd enclaves where Shake 'N' Vac can't easily be sprinkled, then bolt back to their curtain rail sanctuary. I say again, thank goodness Morris is not as delicate as Mrs. Thingy's cats. I shudder to think what Herself would do to if Morris returned to those dark days of 'hide the pongers' that so pungently marked the first three years of his puppyhood. It did the same for our carpet, as I reluctantly recall. Best not to dwell on this. Let's bash the bonfires some more, ay?

OK, then, here's question for you. Why do so many people see fit to celebrate everything remotely noteworthy in their lives, by launching half a ton of ordinance? Why's that then? Time was, only the Queen announced her birthday via organising repeated explosions in a built-up area, but now everyone's at it. Around here, no party is complete without turning Surrey into our little piece of Armageddon, by out-doing the neighbors with louder and more potentially lethal displays of domestic firepower.

It's not as if there isn't an alternative, either. Down the road a piece (I'm talking three miles) is the sprawling splendor of Thorpe Park, where any modern family can enjoy all the queuing, junk food and g-force their bodies can stand, sometimes for as little as a hundred quid. Plus petrol. Oh, and plus the McDonalds' on the way home, just in case there's any danger of you having spare cash to waste on mortgage payments and the like. Anyway, Thorpe Park does the Mother of all fireworks displays, and you can even enjoy it without paying, by parking considerately on the well-tended grass verges of the approach roads. So, as reasonable folks will already see, there is absolutely no need to endanger life, limb, Morris's rest time and Mrs. Thingy's soft furnishings, by turning the rear aspects of our sleepy little hamlet into Cape sodding Kennedy.

Morris was attacked by a rocket last year, you know. Oh yes. Whilst he was spared a direct hit from a dive-bombing missile, he didn't escape an attack from the rear. You see, one of these monsters had run out of fuel somewhere beyond the Crab Nebula, and the spent chassis, complete with splintery stick and shiny red nosecone, had crash-landed due east of Herself's clothes line, causing a seismic shockwave which must have reached nextdoor's new decking at least. The cloud of synthetic volcanic ash thrown up by the impact caused the extinction of an entire woodlouse colony, much the same way as a slightly larger fireball had done for the dinosaurs a few million years ago. Probably.

Next morning, Morris found the rocket and ate most of it, leaving the splintery stick and pointed red nosecone until last. He was about to start on these bits when I found him, looking wretchedly guilty among the hostas. Banished to my office, Morris immediately launched into his celebrated pre-vomit warm up routine. Mouth opened to an impossible angle, lips drawn back to his ears, Morris began to 'bloop-kaarrk!' up a storm. Beyond sympathy, I chivvied him outside, just in time to witness the rocket's second flight, as regurgitated globs of powder-blackened cardboard once more fell to earth.

The vomiting lasted a mere half-hour, but Morris's rear-end fallout, in a vicious parody of bonfire night itself, lasted for days and turned out to be what I've already said it is - a right pain in the arse. I'm with the Mrs. Thingys and Morris's bottoms of this world, and I say that there's a cause ready and waiting for the displaced ladies of Greenham Common. Get your fragrant selves behind the 'Ban The Bonfire' movement, girls - and I'll be right there with you this time.

# Sometimes, All I Need...

## Meet worrying habit no. 2000,006...

Morris has just upped the ante by developing a new habit designed to worry me and wind me up. It's deliberate; oh yes, no doubt about it. As much as such a thing is possible for Morris, he's thought long and hard about this one. He's come up with a real winner, too. In fact, what he's doing now is his best one yet – and I know he knows it.

Over the years, I've had to deal with Morris doing some heavy-duty worry-stuff. He's eaten most of our house and grounds and blocked himself dangerously at both ends with a fair proportion of it. This munch-houses syndrome (do you see what I did there?) has been supported by faked illnesses all over the place, plus he's picked up a sprinkling of pathogens which turned out to be genuine, and of course worrying, and even more of course, expensive. Among a zillion efforts to worry me into an early care home, Morris has flirted with drowning, electrocution, poisoning and imprisonment for shoplifting.

In short, he's been a git. The thing is, I still love him and he knows that, too. This knowledge of my undeserved love is at the root of Morris's latest scheme to wreck my head. His new 'thing' is to...stop breathing. That's what he's doing now. Not-breathing isn't good, is it? Especially the way Morris not-breathes. Like everything else he does, Morris not-breathes with maximum effect, especially on me.

Here's how it works. I'll be in our office (Morris has equal title because his bed's in there and it's where he hides his stash of my underpants and socks – nice) and writing away as I am now in order to keep all manner of wolves from doors. If Morris can't distract me enough and I insist on doing my work, he'll climb onto his bed, sigh theatrically, snuffle and snore a bit to create a bit of noise – then he'll stop breathing to create a seriously scary silence.

As Morris not-breathes, my fingers pause on the keyboard and I listen for the great resumption. Sometimes 30 seconds pass before Morris exhales like a breaching whale and my fingers can once more dance the qwerty tango. Meanwhile, Morris is working up to his next not-breathing episode by doing pantomime yawns with plenty of, frankly unconvincing, smacking of lips.

Sure enough, by way of deliberate contrast to this racket, Morris stops breathing again and what he believes to be a deathly hush, descends once more. I've tried ignoring it and carrying on typing but that's no good at all. Until I can hear him breathing – farting doesn't count, sadly – I absolutely can't write because my mind goes even more blank than normal.

The one thing I daren't do, is turn and look at Morris for visual signs of life. If I do that, he's got me. He'll have won the campaign and not-breathing will be deployed at me for ever more. One of the few consistencies with Morris, is that if his ridiculous behavior gets him attention, it must be worth doing lots more of. I really can't have Morris doing more of this not-breathing lark. The present level of infliction is having a drastic effect on my production and I'm miles behind myself as it is. The fact is, there are a couple of editors threatening to do to me what Morris is doing to himself at the moment. This is not a good environment for a sensitive artiste such as I.

As ever, my strategy must be one of staunch ignorance. That's 'ignore-unce', with the emphasis on the first bit. I don't know how to 'unce', anyway, so I'm sticking with the proven tactics. I've tried banishing Morris to other parts of the house while I work but that never happens for very long. If I'm in our office, Morris must be in here as well. It's the rules. If I try to exclude him, he'll pound on every door in the house until someone (usually Herself, I've noticed) can't stand it any more and lets him into our office.

Turning up my music to block out Morris's mischievous silences is another non-starter and for two unshakable reasons. First, I am a parent and I have the selective hearing that all parents develop which lets us tune in to those we're supposed to be caring for. This is how penguins can find their own chicks in a four-acre mass of fluffy squawking. I'd hear Morris not-breathing no matter how much I pumped up the volume. Anyway, if the music's too loud, Morris barks his stupid head off. So does Herself. Thus, it's the no'est of no-go's.

No, I'll do what I always do at such times. I'll consult my vet, then I'll look for reassurance among my friends and sympathisers. When these measures fail to confirm the normality of what Morris is doing, as they surely will, I'll spread my sad arms toward my virtual chums on the Internet, where I'm sure there must be someone with a positive experience for me to gather.

Meanwhile, I'll just worry myself into dementia and bankruptcy, thanks. Mind you, by the time you read this, Morris may have dispensed with his latest wheeze and all could be productively  tranquil at chez Doe. What's the odds of that happening, then? Don't hold your breath.

# Dopey-Ganger?

## It's finally happened. I've become Morris...

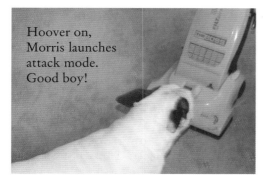

Hoover on, Morris launches attack mode. Good boy!

You know the old saying about owners looking like their dogs? Well, I think Morris and I have a bit of that going on. Confused demeanor, waddling gait and impression of latent sinister tendencies aside, we don't so much look alike as act in a similar stylie. In fact, now I really think about it, Morris and I are increasingly functioning as one.

For a start, we hate the vacuum cleaner with a passion. I've yet to attack the hideous creature with jaws a'slaver as Morris prefers, but I despise it every bit as much as he does. We loathe its droning intrusion and the way it forces us to abandon comfortable places and postures we've worked for hours to perfect. We deeply resent that Hoover's right to roam and its priority within this household.

We've been turfed off sofas by the whining dirt-sucker. We are regularly chivvied from carpets when our backs have been pressed against deliciously warm radiators whilst cushions pillow our heads and the Discovery Channel fills them with interesting things about sharks and Hitler. We are even evicted from our very own office, and banished until the mechanical maidservant has clattered over every tile and thrust its flexible proboscis into our secret crannies in search of illegal fluff, hairs and dust. We absolutely hate that Hoover. That's why neither of us ever uses it. We have our principles, Morris and I.

We also share an overwhelming desire to howl and snarl when selfish gits invade our lifespace with fireworks. You'll be reading this article early in the new year, which these days means that you're already likely to be caught in the run-up to bonfire night, so you'll know what Morris and I are talking about. Oh yes, before the flask-size shells of their New Year fireworks have even cooled in your gardens, the fuses will be smouldering on the next salvo of pet-shattering explosives. At the moment, the fireworks-inspired fear-poo on our carpets all belongs to Morris, but rage and terror are the closest of cousins and that situation could well change. I'll then tell Herself not to blame Morris and me, but to please let us out of his kennel and direct her rage toward the backyard bombadiers that caused the trouble in the first place. She'll almost listen, too.

# A Guide Dog For The Thick

My dog and I tread spookily similar paths along health's highway. Whenever one of us is ill, the other's life is affected by the fallout. Morris recently had some intestinal syndrome or other which turned his colon into a snow-blower. Sadly, it wasn't snow that his colon was blowing but a drift of semi-digested dog food, plus whatever he'd managed to steal. Although it was definitely Morris that was ill, such is our symbiosis that it was me that was sick every time the snow hit the fan. As always at times of Morris's gastro-gymnastics, I'm condemned to follow his every move and cart him outside as soon as I see his 'blower' kick into gear.

Now, on the rare occasions when I'm allowed an illness, Morris follows me around all over the place like some piggy-eyed minder. He'll accompany me to the loo if I don't hoik him outside, and even then I can't concentrate on being ill in the toilet because Morris is sitting on the other side of the door, doing his anguished sighing bit. We're an 'in sickness and in health' item, Morris and I.

Yet more samenesses include a love of sprawling on soft furnishings to watch sport and nature documentaries, a hatred of anything soap, Pop Idol, Big Brother or I'm Terminally Tragic Get Me Out Of Here, plus a healthy adoration of Nigella. I know Morris shares my views on these things because he drools when I drool, and leaves the room with me when dross comes on the telly that my lot claim to enjoy.

We're also mutual morning guys. We're up and about at 5 a.m., tapping our six feet to the rhythm of the new day, as we stride across the world on walkies patrol. We're the only 'morning' people in our entire family. If work and school didn't crowbar them into action, the rest would fester in their pits until their bladders dragged them to the bog. Morris and I look down our combined noses at such a shameful waste of daylight and attack its shuffling wasters with deliberate cheerfulness. We smile, whistle, sing wrongly-worded bits of current pop songs (kids hate it when you do that – it's great) and generally caper about like the wee scamps we are. Together. As one. That's one man and his dog, and vice-versa.

Sometimes it's hard to see where Morris ends and I begin. Perhaps we were each other in a former life. Maybe we're spiritually linked, and will haunt this earth in various forms for eternity. Perhaps I'm just really, really stupid. And that, dear readers, would be yet another thing my dog and I have in common.

Well, that's it for Book One. Rest assured though, Morris will make certain that there's *more* than enough material for a follow-up.

Until then, then.